A Testimony of Victory
Making it through Trying Times

Ethel G. Wade

Kingdom Builders Publications LLC

This Book Belongs to

A Testimony of Victory: Making it through Trying Times
Copyright © 2016 by Ethel G. Wade
Kingdom Builders Publications

All rights reserved. No part of this book may be reproduced or transmitted in any form or by any means without written permission from the author.

ISBN 13: 978-0-692-67772-8
Library of Congress Control Number: 2016937190

All Scripture used are from the King James Version

Story by
Ethel (Effia Mae) Gordon Wade
Narrated by
Louise James
Editor
Wanda Brown
Cover Designer
LoMar Designs
Photographer
L H Photography

Printed in USA
Go to our website: www.kingdombuilderspublications.com

Ethel G. Wade

DEDICATION

This book is dedicated to the loving memory of my great grandmother, Rosetta Ross Grant, whom we affectionately called Granny. She instilled in me, the principle of faith in God. Through her life, living and sacrifices, Granny set a foundation for my life, which included honesty and hard work. I am so grateful for the faith she imparted in me at an early age. She taught me to trust in the Lord Jesus. I trust Him for my strength, believing that he will never leave me nor forsake me.

I thank God for my loving husband of 59 years, Cary Wade Sr., who stood by my side through the good and bad. He supported me, sometimes without a word; but standing by gingerly as my quiet storm. I thank God that he chose me, and his humbleness and willingness proves his love for me. We learned to stand together in all situations. He's my friend, partner, and confidant.

I also dedicate this book to my brother, Johnny Lee, and to the memory of my darling deceased sister Lucille; to my four wonderful and darling children, our 12 grandchildren, 13 great grandchildren, and to those to come (our crowns, **Proverbs 17:6**).

I thank Kingdom Builders Publications and above all, I thank God for divinely influencing me to write.

As I sat alone one Saturday night, a thought came to me, *write your story, and do not despise your youth!* Then the

Scripture came to mind, **1 Timothy 4:12,** *"Let no man despise thy youth; but be thou an example of the believers, in word, in conversation, in charity, in spirit, in faith, in purity."* From that point, I began putting my life on tape. For 25 years, this work has been in the making and finally my story is penned. I pray the divinely inspired pages of my story and the wisdom and knowledge of my life experiences will touch you and increase your faith in God.

As I think about this book, two passages of Scriptures come to mind. The first is **3 John 1:3**, which says, *3 For I rejoiced greatly, when the brethren came and testified of the truth that is in thee, even as thou walkest in the truth.*

The second passage is from **Revelation 12:11**, which says, *11 And they overcame him by the blood of the Lamb, and by the word of their testimony; and they loved not their lives unto the death.*

May this book bless you as much as I've been blessed by writing it.

Ethel G. Wade

CONTENTS

	Dedication	iv
	Acknowledgements	7
	Introduction	8
1	MOVING	12
2	HARD TIMES	23
3	FAMILY TIES	42
4	MARRIAGE	47
5	MY THREE AUNTS	58
6	MASSIVE STRUGGLE	60
7	MICHAEL	78
8	KNOWLEDGE OF GENERATIONAL CURSES	94
9	MY YOUNG ADULTS	103
10	BROTHER RETURNS HOME	118
11	UNITY	121
12	SHOP – JOB – CHURCH AND TEMPTATION	125
13	REVELATIONS AND PRAYERS	147
	EPILOGUE	153
	MORE ABOUT THE AUTHOR	154
	REVELENCE OF THREE'S: MY TESTIMONY	156
	A DUAL CAREER CHRISTIAN MARRIAGE	159
	SIX STEPS TO SALVATION	162

ACKNOWLEDGMENTS

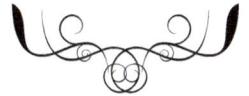

I acknowledge the many people who made an impact on my life and the making of my testimony.

I would like to acknowledge and thank three women who encouraged and helped me, Minister Rosemary Griffin, Sister Carolyn Stroman, and Sister Pat Glaston. After hearing a little bit of my story, they strongly encouraged me to write.

I thank God for the trials and tribulations He allowed me to suffer and endure because they helped make me a living testimony.

To God be the Glory.

Ethel G. Wade

INTRODUCTION

My parents, Freddie Gordon and Rosetta Jamison, were united in holy matrimony on March 24, 1937. From this union three children were born. Johnny Lee Gordon was the oldest, born on December 11, 1937. Lucille Gordon was born on December 1, 1938, and I was born on November 6, 1939. My mother's demise came well before our mature years were realized.

The great city of Livingston sits in Orangeburg County and is sandwiched between Norway and North in South Carolina. This was our home. We were told that our mother expired on March 25, 1942 after childbirth, eight months shy of my third birthday. Most families in those days took care of family members or anyone who was in distress or trouble. Such was the case with our family. A cousin took us in her home and cared for us while our father worked as a carpenter at Fort Jackson Army Base in Columbia, South Carolina. Johnny remembered more about our father than Lucille and me. We knew nothing about our mother and very little about our father's lineage, except the stories close relatives shared with us.

Not long after our mother passed, our father remarried. His new wife came with four children of her own and instantly we became a family of nine. Johnny was such a tenderhearted fellow. Things seemed to hurt him deeply. He was affected by most things and internalized practically everything; never openly expressing how or what he felt. Before we could get adjusted to what seemed like a positive change in our lives, tragedy struck again. I was feeling good about our new big family for love and support. Then mid-March 1945, father fell from a tall building while working and was critically injured. He died four months later, July 1, 1945, from his injuries. Father's death was a major setback for my brother because he and dad were inseparable. He followed dad everywhere. Johnny withdrew and mourned deeply, and cried himself to sleep many nights. Being the youngest, I didn't understand what was going on.

We were left alone; both biological parents gone from us permanently. The devastation of loss is a life changer, but to lose both parents when we were so young is something so unimaginable! No one should ever have to experience that kind of loss, yet we survived without a costly backlash. We remained with father's wife afterwards, however she made the situation worse by telling a family member she was not able to care for seven children. This was a tremendous blow.

A few weeks following, God sent a visitor. She was very small in stature, a sweetly petite and elderly lady who came to see us. She was about 5 feet, 4 inches tall and soft spoken. She didn't look or act her age. Her skin and mannerisms were that of a much younger woman, but Mrs. Ross was 74 years of age at the time. She told us that we were going home with her; she was going to be our new momma. Her hometown was Norway, South Carolina. She took us home to live with her on a farm. We later learned that this old lady was our great grandmother. Her name was Rosetta Grant Ross, but we called her granny. There was an older person closer to our age living with her. He was our cousin Tommy Ross and he was twelve years old. There was also an older grandson, our mother's half-brother, Odell. He and his family helped Granny run the farm. They lived in their own house on the same farm not far from Granny. This was quite a change for three young children! Granny was a lively stone. She had tenacity, fervor, strength, a strong resolve, a hard work ethic like no other person I had ever seen, which would take us through the next 11 years of our lives.

Granny Rosetta was a farmer from her heart. She lived in an old farmhouse that had quaint little front and back porches, two bedrooms, living room and kitchen. The four children slept in one bedroom and Granny slept in the other. Living with Granny gave us security and a sense of love, and after what we had gone through, we were ready to be filled with love again. Since we wanted to get love and give love, Granny and Cousin Tommy became our mother and father figures. Although, Tommy was close in age to us, he was quite mature and responsible for his age. We fell in love with them in no time because we needed someone to talk to, play with and care for us. Despite our new stable family, Johnny still spent many nights crying and that caused me to cry.

To add to our burden, our sister Lucille was

intellectually challenged along with a speech impediment. Because of the communication deficiency, she enormously suffered with new people. Her social and intellectual challenges made it virtually impossible for her to adjust to different situations or people. We were ill-prepared as children to help her, but we watched over her the best we could. However, I didn't realize that Johnny would need me in his later teenage years too.

Through every trial and triumph Johnny, Lucille and I remained a close-knit family. Regardless of the milestones we faced, we did it with dignity, unity and by the principles set by our Granny's example. We unfolded family secrets, overcame struggles and challenges over many years.

This is my memory from Granny's history engraved forever on the tablets of my heart. She taught us to pray and to have faith in God. Although the Negros had limited resources and options, she persevered, showing us anything is possible and we could excel at anything. In her tender way to relieve the pain, and to make our chores a little easier, or perhaps to take our mind off our fears, she bought us a little red wagon. This was not a toy, but transportation for the cotton. We had to fill the farm wagon several times a day and at the end of the day, our pay came. We were grateful for what Granny gave us.

Ethel G. Wade

MOVING
CHAPTER ONE

Granny controlled our childhood energies by keeping us busy. We were given more chores to do. Rosetta Grant was a woman of great family pride and she took great pride in her beloved farm animals. Granny owned hogs and chickens, so she gave us an important job of minding them. This was one of the many chores we had to do around the farm house. Granny sold eggs and young pigs to help along the way. Granny was a proud woman. Although she desperately needed public assistance, she didn't believe in a hand out from the state or government and would not accept any help from the State for us.

Granny worked hard but never got fair pay for her hard work. Many times, she sold her goods and was cheated out of a fair price. I would cry myself to sleep at night hoping she would accept some type of help for us so she would not have to work so hard, but she wouldn't. She taught us how to work and not to depend on anyone.

Granny was firm. When she said yes, it was yes and when she said no, it was no. We knew never to debate or sass her. She would say, "Listen and you shall learn." We listened attentively although she repeatedly gave one lesson again and again. She was very careful in teaching us the wiles and dangers we might face while doing chores.

On the farm, sometimes we had to go in wooded areas to get the hogs when they got out the pen. Recovering them, Lucille would help guide them back to the pen. We were often bruised from brier bushes while trying to help.

All the time she would warn us about the dangerous animals that we might face around the farm such as the poison red belly lizards, the black snakes and the rattlesnakes. She would say, "The black snake will run on his tail and if he catches you, he will wrap himself around you and put his tail up your nose to see if you are still breathing." Then he will beat you until you stop breathing!" However, she said the rattlesnake is the most dangerous one of all in this part of the country. "He will never bother you unless you get too close to him, touch something he's on, or get close enough for him to smell you."

Now I was really scared. At least twice a week, my brother, cousins, and I went down to the edge of the woods to gather wood for heating and cooking. However,

Granny made sure that we knew about anything lurking in the woods of danger. She would make us sit down and listen, as she would teach us about the dangers on the farm, mainly about the rattlesnake. She would say if we ever walked up on one and see him before he strikes you, (if he's on your right) don't run left, nor go forward. Granny insisted that we move slowly backwards, the same way we came in and we would not be bothered. Lord, I didn't know how to believe what she was telling us concerning the rattlesnake, but I'm so grateful that I listened to that old woman. Later in life, her words would save my life from a 13-year-old rattlesnake.

The fall of 1946, we enrolled in our first school, Norway Elementary. My first teacher was Mrs. Mary Tyler Robinson. I will never forget her because she gave me a good start in life. Mrs. Robinson was much like our Granny. She did not spare the rod on her pupils. Granny taught us our teachers were our parents away from home and we must respect them the same as we respected her. Not only was Mrs. Robinson my mother away from home, but she was also my mentor. I loved her and respected her as such. She never held back from chastening me when she felt I needed it. The discipline made me respect her even more. I knew what I would get if I did not follow her instructions. I enjoyed being in her class. The time we spent in school was very precious to us.

My brother Johnny enjoyed about four years of school. He spent a lot of working on the farm helping Uncle Odell. Johnny took advantage of bad weather days to go to school. Due to Lucille's challenges, I would go with her to her class and talk for her so that her teacher would understand what she was trying to say. My brother and I loved Lucille and did everything we could for her. My brother was very attentive to both of us when he was permitted to go to school. Johnny did his very best and we loved our brother for all he did.

Granny loved farming and Tommy hated farming. She worked the mule like Tommy and worked Tommy like the mule. Three years later after the death of our parents, Granny came for us to live with her. We were too young for farm work at that time, but we did have chores. Two years later in 1947 my brother, age ten had to learn the farm work from Uncle and his sons. This is when Tommy saw his way out so he confided in us that secretly he was planning to leave Granny and the hard farm work. I could only imagine how hard it was being a regular teenager, working like Pharaoh's slave, and dealing with Granny's strong opinions and pride. I believe he loved helping his beloved Granny. I am sure he didn't want to leave that good cooking and good loving. We tried to convince him not to leave, but Cousin Tommy left anyway in 1947 after the crop gathering season was over, just before my brother's 10th birthday.

Granny and Uncle Odell diligently looked for him around town and other farm communities but could not find him anywhere. Now our uncle had become our father and his sons were like brothers to us. We all were hurt by Tommy's leaving, but my brother took it the hardest. Not long after, Johnny went through withdrawals. He would only talk when spoken to, and then responded with very few words.

We were really going through tough times. Nothing was stable in our lives. Every time we turned around, it seemed someone was leaving us. We saw Tommy only once after he left home, which was in North, South Carolina. By this time, he was a grown man. We never saw him again.

Uncle Odell and his sons lived about one mile from Granny. He and his sons were now Granny's main help on the farm. They told my brother that one day they were going to teach him to work on the farm and how to plow a mule. Johnny was a good listener, a very humble person, and a quick learner. Uncle would try to persuade Granny to give up farming so that she could get some assistance for us, but she refused to hear anything about getting help from the State. She would say, "Johnny will learn to work the farm soon; I won't need any help for them." Many good people would talk to her about state assistance but she was not hearing it. Knowing that she had a hard row to hoe, the kind people of our community came and helped where they could, including donating some hand-me-down clothes. Her children would give her things for us as well.

Granny was a church-going, Bible believing woman and she believed the Lord was going to make a way for us. She taught us how to respect ourselves and others. This was one of the foundations and her heart's cry. Granny made sure we got to church every Sunday for Sunday school even if we had to walk or go in the wagon. Church going, we didn't mind at all, we just didn't want go in the wagon.

Granny prayed with and for us, that God would strengthen and keep us. I thank God, she was a spiritual woman. She gave us hope, never letting us forget the LORD was our help through mankind!

Granny taught us to be obedient to all people. Granny would say, "Always treat them the way we wanted them to treat us." She would pray for others as she prayed with us by her side every morning and night. She would tell us not to worry about what others had, but to be thankful for what we had. She explained the word to us from her God-given wisdom. Granny was not able to read the bible but she quoted parts of Bible Scriptures throughout the 11 years she kept us.

Granny had great wisdom from above and she shared it with us. I thank God to this day for her. She made me a good listener.

Christmas for us was never full of luxuries because we were very poor. We would find in our little hats on Christmas morning a few pieces of candy, two oranges, a few nuts, and two apples. However, the Christmas of 1947, our second Christmas with Granny, Lucille and I were lucky. We got one little white clay doll to share. Granny said, "Be thankful for what you get, because the real meaning of Christmas is to love Jesus; it's His birthday." She would tell us as long as we had a shelter over our head, food on our table, clothes on our back and shoes on our feet, we were more than blessed. It was hard for us to understand what she was saying at that time. Sometimes we would get very angry because we had so much to do and got so little in return. Granny would say, "Every little bit helps and the Lord will look out for His children."

In January of 1948, our uncle and his family had to move because he had conflicts with his boss the year before, so Granny had to follow. Uncle Odell and his family were the main source of her help on the farm, so we had to move too. Again, we left school mid-year. I hated it because we had finally settled in at Norway Elementary. I knew I was losing friends and a good motherly teacher in Mrs. Robinson.

Our Second Move

We moved near a little town named Nesses, South Carolina. We thought this would be a good move because Uncle and Granny wanted to rent with the possibility to own someday. Granny had high hopes of buying this little piece of land. Q Granny's house had two small bedrooms, a large living room and kitchen, and a large front porch. We had to make a path to walk about through the house during cotton picking season.

Granny was a strong disciplinary. She said she was tough on us because she loved us. I see now what she was saying, love is seeing a problem, and doing something about it, as Jesus did for the whole world. Scripture says, *"For God so love the world that he gave his only begotten son! That whosoever believes in him shall not perish, but have everlasting life!"*

We didn't understand that chastening was love at the time. In our minds, it almost seemed as if she didn't love us because spankings hurt so much. She didn't spare the rod at all because she loved us. What a blessing! She was doing what the Bible said we must do if we love our children. **Proverbs 13:24** says, *"He that spares his rod hates his son, "but he that loves him chastened him in *betimes"* (early). When Granny promised us a beating we would get it. Her caring for us made us know how to respect ourselves, especially our elders.

Soon we were enrolled in the new school, Sand Hill Elementary in Neeses, South Carolina. Of course, by moving in the middle of the school year, I had to repeat the second grade. Unfortunately, Johnny, Lucille and I attended school more on the days it rained, much like every other farming family in our rural town because farming was impossible during bad weather.

Our institution of learning was a little old boarded schoolhouse, shy of paint inside and out, with two rooms and no windows. When we had to relieve ourselves, one of the two teachers would assist or chaperone us to the outhouse. Our teacher was nice enough, although I don't remember her at length. Classes were small because every farming family had sons and daughters who would help with farming, so on rainy days attendance would be much greater.

The rain and sun did its miracle work on the ground. Granny planted her special space called "big garden." This portion was for her family. She would hoe up bunches of grass and we would shake the dirt off the grass so it would die to prepare her garden. However, after doing this work for a while, God did the miraculous again, and everything was looking better. The girls did the big garden and the boys did the whole field, but Granny did them both.

Granny also planted cotton which grew well. She taught us how to hoe the cotton without chopping it up. When the cotton was ready, we picked it and drug it back to the house. Granny used the porch and part of the living room to store the cotton until we picked a whole bale.

Granny taught us how to till the ground. For the Big garden, she and I did it completely with our hands. Uncle taught Johnny how to use the plow and till a field with a mule. One of the most pitiful sights to see was my brother toe to toe with a plow almost as tall as him. Most times when he started to till the ground, he would fall down many times, but he was determined to keep that plow upright. With determination and hard work, he got the job done.

Johnny was still very introverted and wouldn't say too much about what he was going through, but I always knew his heart. I candidly talked to him about things we had to do. I felt sorry for him because he didn't go to school as much as I went. My heart broke for him when I thought of his plight.

My Granny said when we were younger that God would take care of us, and what do you know, we came onto a land of milk and honey. This farm had a tree archery. There were grapevines, peach trees, pear trees and apple trees. We loved the fruits even though we had to fight the bees to eat them. We'd come to love the new land and prayed we could remain on it. Other than the hard work and the very small house, it seemed to be a blessing.

Unfortunately, it wasn't meant to be, December 1949, our uncle broke bad news that he had to move again. Granny was very upset. She didn't want to move this time at all. Nonetheless, she knew we had to. There were several reasons why she couldn't stay. First, our brother was not old enough to care for the farm alone. Secondly, we needed a bigger house. Thirdly, Johnny needed his own space because he was now 12. Sister was 11, and I was 10. Granny needed more space for the three growing preteens. She told us this would be the last time we would have to move. Johnny, with our help, would be able to handle the farm alone if Uncle moved again. I was so glad to hear that because I was tired of moving from house to house and farm to farm, dealing with all the changes.

This was our third exhausting move since the death of our mother in 1942.

We finally found out why Uncle moved every two years. He and his sons were working so hard every year caring for both farms (Granny's and his) but they would never clear any money at the end of the year. The owner told Uncle Odell he broke even and would lend him a little piece of money to get him over until the next year. He would never profit anything with six children. Uncle was heartbroken, furious, and outraged and he spoke his mind. Yet, Granny would never say too much. She would just pray that the next year would be better. They were treated so unfairly and as a result, so were we. After all, we were assisting them in doing the work. We worked so hard with little or nothing to show for our hard work.

Granny didn't have to buy much food because she supplemented her income with her big garden and stock she would sell. She grew her own sugar cane to make her own syrup, and she had her corn grind for grits. The most of what Granny had to buy was rice, flour, and any other grain necessary for cooking. Farming was her heart during the 11 years we lived with her, and family connection was her heart's desire.

HARD TIMES
CHAPTER TWO

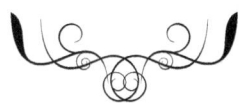

Finding a Family member 1950 – 1955

Granny found a larger house, thank goodness. This house was on the Fillmore place, located between Norway and Cope, South Carolina. This house had two bedrooms, a large living room, kitchen, and dining room. Granny used the dining room for my brother's bedroom. Now he had his own bedroom for the first time. Lucille and I had our room and Granny had hers. The house also had a small storage room on the front porch that Granny used to store her canned goods. She canned everything she could including the sausage and pudding made from the hogs she killed.

For the little schooling my brother would receive, Granny made certain we were enrolled in school at Good Hope Elementary between Norway and Cope, South Carolina. I was held back again because of the timing of our move. I didn't matriculate to the fourth grade. How disappointing to be sent back to the third grade. Now I was two years behind my class. This was such a hurting feeling but I just wanted to go to school and wanted to be there every day if I could. It hurt me when they told my Granny that my sister Lucille wouldn't attend school after the second term at that school because of her special circumstance. The school didn't have a specialist to work with her, so she could no longer attend.

Uncle and his family were still helping her, within walking distance from us. That was good for us. There were other families living on this farm. The James', the Ryant's, the Curry's, the Darby's, and the Mack family all pitched in with food, clothing, etc. to help out the family. The comradery was so delightful. Neighboring was a lot like ants in their colonies. Working diligently and selflessly to accomplish the common good for everyone involved. These beautiful families helped raise and support each other's children, and when I tell you there were a lot of children, it was like the heritage of Abraham and the sand; children for days! Wherever there is a multiplicity of children, the great thing about it is, you can always find your age group to share things with, and that was a blessing. The Ryant's children, Clyde, Ruby, and Bettie were like our own sisters and brothers. They were Granny's children at our house and we were their parent's children to them at their house. If we got into trouble, we would get the switch, then when the switching news got to our Granny we received a double portion. We all became the best of friends. It was a great, happy time, but it was more than happiness, we all were filled with joy.

Johnny made it to the beginning of his teenage years, and Lucille and I were right behind. Johnny was consumed with the notion that Granny would have him run the farm alone. That idea terrified him and made him worry. Although we felt like we were in the lap of luxury with the fruit archery, the grounds were not very different from the previous farms. This farm had the same kind of sorry patches of Johnson, Mutter, and Nut grass in the field as the other farm. Here we go again...clearing all over again.

On this farm, Granny Ross was sharecropping again. She bought a mule and a cow which gave us more chores. Did Granny think we didn't have enough chores to do with all the house and farm work? We had to take care of a mule and cow. Lord, I remember it so vividly, drawing water from the well to water the livestock. The mule we called Lottie and the cow was Bettie. Now and again they would get out the pen. My brother could call them by name and they'd come. Most of the time they'd wander off and Johnny would look for them. Lucille and I would find Bettie the cow because her wandering skills were not mature at all. She'd go no further than the next green pasture. You couldn't tell Bettie the grass was not greener on the other side because she was grazing her time away until we found her.

Granny was aging but she could still get around well. We were still trying to attend school every day we could. Johnny made his resolve to stay home to watch uncle and his sons on the farm. Thanks to God Uncle and his sons were still with us. I would come home in the afternoon and see Brother trying to hold the plow to turn the land. Uncle, his sons, and my brother would work from sunrise to sunset. Through the grueling work, Johnny in his exhaustion, still help to feed the mule and cow. Johnny was so tired from a day's work until he could sleep like a hibernating bear, and still wake up saturated with fatigue. I felt such compassion for my brother's heart. He worked so hard and was still so young. Johnny was quite an intelligent young man, he caught on to things very quickly. In some of our brother and sister talks, we'd talk about learning responsibility. The experiences we had in life helped us tremendously.

Granny had a daughter living in Orangeburg, South Carolina. Her name was Cora. Granny wanted me to go and help Aunt Cora some weekends because she wasn't always in her best health. This was like Christmas to me on a hot, summer's day. It was summer of 1952 and I was twelve years old. I was changing; my body was becoming a young lady. I was at the age where I wanted to meet and talk with other girls my age or older. We had close friends we could go and play with around the farm, but I loved meeting new people. I was excited to visit Aunt Cora. I enjoyed helping people, and helping Aunt Cora gave me a pass to rest from the hard labor of my precious, hard hitting, stone of a woman Granny. I would have loved for my beautiful sister to come along to Aunt Cora's house, but because of her ill-adjustment to new people and her inability to speak well, I made the choice not to put her in an embarrassing situation. Lucille couldn't help that she was unable to communicate like the other girls, but I gave her everything I saw and felt. We shared everything, every moment and detail.

The weekend had come and Uncle and Granny took me to help Aunt Cora. She mentioned having a friend who was a teacher. Her name was Mrs. Lawrence and she had a boarding house for young college girls while they attended school. Aunt Cora said, "You being a good talker, when you finish your work, you can go over and meet the young girls. That way you'll have someone to associate with when you're visiting me here in Orangeburg." After finishing my work for Aunt Cora that Sunday afternoon, Aunt Cora and I walked towards Claflin College where Mrs. Lawrence's boarding house was. I was very excited to meet her and the girls at her boarding home. She introduced me to the young ladies. They were all very friendly. Although this was my first time meeting them, it was as if we had known each other for years. After talking awhile, something happened that completely blew my mind. I met a girl who was my father's relative. I had hope to meet someone kin to my Dad because I'd been searching a long time. Imagine my elation. Her name is Stella Inabinet from my Dad's hometown, Livingston, SC. As we embraced, I could hardly hold back my tears. To my astonishment, she felt the same as me and I was overjoyed to finally find one of my father's aunt's granddaughter. I didn't want to turn her a loose. I could hardly wait to get home and tell Johnny and Lucille I had found my father's cousin, Florence Inabinet's daughter Stella. I was able to contact my father's brother through her. My siblings and I started finding more of my father's family members. What a blessing this was. God's mighty hands was moving in my life again all because I was willing to work to help my elders. To God be the glory! That Sunday afternoon was a joyful time; a time I will never forget! Especially remembering the expressions on the faces of my siblings that night.

Afterward, I found my Uncle Earnest and his family. They lived in Philadelphia, PA. After finding out about Uncle Earnest and his family, we stayed in touch with them by phone. After a while he came down to visit us at Granny's house. Uncle Earnest promised us that only death would separate us from him again. He stuck to his promise. Lucille even got a chance to stay with him for a year in Philadelphia. Thanks to him and his family, we met many other family members.

Back on the Farm

Six O'clock early Monday morning, while the smile is still fresh on my face from the day before; when God gave me his choice blessing for ministering to my Aunt Cora, the family gathered for breakfast. Now it's back in the field again hoeing and pulling up weeds. My smile was quickly turned into seven acres of dread looking over the field. We would do this for days until we covered the whole seven acres of cotton and corn field checking for every spot of bad grass we could find. Once a week, we knocked off early to haul wood for Granny. Johnny and I would go to this old abandoned sawmill in the farm wagon. There was a lot of old 2x4 plywood that Granny used for heating and cooking. We had the same routine just about every weekend. Johnny would leave the wagon a little distance from the wood pile and we would carry the wood to the wagon. However, on this particular day, Granny Ross's words came to pass.

That Big RATTLE SNAKE

As I bent down to pick up the wood, I heard a rattling sound to the right of me it sounded like rocks shaking in a bag. I held my breath slowly to my right I saw the biggest rattlesnake in my life, shaking his rattles, ready to strike! We had no business in that old abandoned building. We were in Snake territory, this was his land and we were indeed trespassing. I became so numb, I felt paralyzed. However, it was NO time for frozen fear or drawing a blank. I had to get it together fast and bring back those words of Granny. Johnny didn't know what was happening, he just kept yelling, "Pick up the wood, Mae." My mind thawed out enough for the memory of Granny's words. I was not to run to my left nor forward, if the snake was on my right; and the snake was indeed on my right. I was told to back out the same way I came in, and I did. I must have done the 90-yard dash in 2.5 seconds. While escaping with a fastest sprint I could muster, I didn't think I had time to warn my brother, but while doing the dash, I was yelling SNAKE, SNAKE. I ran all the way home, up that hill and down that road, and fell on the porch. Granny saw me come in a dash and questioned, "What's the matter?" Panting profusely, "Snake! Snake!" I exclaimed. Johnny came shortly behind me with the farm wagon, went for his shot gun, and back to the wood pile. The snake was still there in his striking position and had not moved as Granny said. My brother killed that snake and brought the snake home. He sported that snake around on Granny's car in the neighborhood. That snake had 13 rattles on its tail, with moss down his back. What a coincidence! I was thirteen years old at the time this incident occurred. Thank God I listened to that old woman's teaching, although many times I didn't want too! My life was saved that day because of her teaching.

Granny believed in God, and taught us the importance of attending church. I can remember her saying that her heart belonged to God. She taught us that God is love; He is a father to the fatherless, and a mother to the motherless. "You will always have a friend in Jesus," she would say, he is a friend in deed, she thanked and praised the Lord for saving her child's life. I found out she was quoting parts of **Jeremiah 17:14** which reads, *"Heal me, O Lord, and I shall be healed; Save me, and I shall be saved, for you are my praise."* Yes, he saved my life that day and many times after and I can truly say he is my Savior. Yes, she gave the Lord all the glory… for my life, although I was almost too breathless to hear her, I just thank God for making me a good listener.

Our Church worship service was on the first and third Sundays of the month. This was the house of worship where we felt safe from all troubles. Living on the Fillmore Farm near our church, Good Hope AME, located near Cope, we were close enough to walk to church and that is just what we had to do many times. Cars would pass us on the dusty dirt roads. It was embarrassing for us to have to walk and see other people riding in their cars. Sometimes we would get picked up by someone who was nice enough to do so. Thank goodness! We would leave early for Sunday school. Granny would be picked up by Uncle or a neighbor at times for services because she was not able to walk to church. There were times when she couldn't get a ride to church and Johnny would have to bring her with the mule and farm wagon. Lucille and I would ride in the farm wagon part of the way and we would jump off and walk the rest of the way, when Granny allowed us to. Johnny would be so ashamed when he had to come to church with the mule and wagon but we had no choice. We were obedient to Granny and did what we were told. We knew we had to go to church Sunday School unless it rained or there was sickness.

By the fall of 1953, Uncle Odell had to move again. He left us with Granny on this farm. He felt we were old enough to run the farm at 16, 15 and fourteen. After bad weather, there was no work to be done on the farm. We ourselves had many acres of land to care for besides our house work and big garden. I remember vividly seeing that old blue and green pickup coming down that dirt road. I would dread it so much because I knew it was the white man coming to get us to gather their vegetation or pick cotton. Granny could say no sometime but she didn't know how to say no as long as the weather was suitable. So, on our rest days from bad weather, they'd come for

Aunt Rosetta; my Granny. The driver would let her sit in the front seat of that old pickup while we'd ride on the back going to help pick peas, butter beans, cucumbers, watermelons, cantaloupes and whatever else needed to be picked on their farm. Sometimes on Saturday mornings, we would pick cotton, which provided a little extra money for us for the weekend. Johnny and I would pick a hundred pounds of cotton by noon on Saturday. We were being paid two dollars for every hundred pounds we picked. Out of the two dollars, Granny would allow us to keep half of it. She would say that it was too much money to waste up, so we surrendered humbly our hard-earned money. During the summer, when there was hardly nothing to do on the farm, Johnny would work for Bossman, helping to put up fences and whatever else they had to do. After a hard week of laboring and keeping everything in order, the only way we had to get to town was to catch Bossman's truck. Every Saturday afternoon, the truck would come through the community. Everybody who needed transportation to town would catch this truck.

We got groceries at the Bossman's store. At the end of every year, Granny barely came out of debt. Most of the time, Bossman would say she just broke even, no matter how good the crop was. Granny Ross used to say, "Having your own mule is like having your own tractor." She would encourage us to take care of that mule because he would save us money at the end of the crop year. We should have something left over at the end of the year because Bossman said half of the crop was hers, minus food, seeds, and fertilizer. His math was certainly different than ours, especially at the end of crop year. Also, Granny was told that she was going to get half of what the crop made, which would allow her to buy us some of the things we wanted, and I wanted a sofa chair for the living room. She always tried to give us hope.

By the spring of 1954, we had additional work to do on this farm. More hardship for us in getting the soil ready. We had to take the manure from the stable where the cow and mule were kept. We would put it on the wagon twice or three times a day to fertilize the land. We would spread it as far as it could go. We did this the spring of 1954 and 1955. Granny would say the manure was to the soil like vitamins to the human body, but Lord it was stink. Johnny and I didn't like to do this kind of work at all. It was embarrassing and smelly. The summer was cotton blooming season. However, the boll weevils had gotten so bad on the cotton that the cotton had to be poisoned. Bossman gave Granny some poison syrup to put on the cotton since she didn't have the money to pay the man to poison the cotton with the tractor, even though it was his farm. So, Johnny used a piece of board about two and a half feet long. He put a jar at each end of the board and drilled holes in the top of the jars. We filled the jars with the poison syrup. The board was just as long as the cotton rows were wide apart. Johnny, Lucille, and I would take two rows at a time each. The three of us would walk up and down the rows of cotton with the poison syrup pouring from the top of the jars onto the cotton stocks. We did this until we finished five acres of cotton. For my sister and me to be young women, we had to do a lot of masculine work.

Granny would also help Lucille with her part in poisoning the cotton. Even though Granny couldn't go like Johnny or me, we were blessed for what she did. We would tell her how hard the work was and she would say, "The Lord is going to help you to grow into a strong woman and man. You will know how to make an honest and decent living to support your own family someday if it's the good Lord's will." She always reminded us that anything that comes too easy is no good. She would say, "If you work hard for something, you'll always enjoy it better."

Granny would talk to us every chance she could about things that we needed to know or might have a question about. I was curious about many things. It bothered me that we couldn't afford to dress like other children because I liked this young man. I wanted Granny to be able to get me some nice clothing, but I was thankful to have those mothers on the farm who gave us nice things to help Granny. My spirit was lifted when I was told things won't be this way always. Things were going to get better. It was a blessing having these other mothers to talk to. They would say some of the same things Granny told us. Granny often said, "Don't worry about what others are wearing, because it's not what the person is wearing that counts." She would say, "Wear what you have with pride and the good Lord will provide." Seeing our neighbor's children going to school on a regular basis would make me very sad. I always talked to Granny about school. She would say, "Mae, you may not have a whole lot of education but the Lord is going to use you wisely with what you got." She would say "Mae, with the good Lord working through you, you will be able to do more than some with a lot of education." Often, she would say this to me, but I didn't understand what she was saying at that time. I just listened to her and hoped for the best. Today, I truly can say that I understand what she was saying to me.

For it is not you who speaks, but the Spirit of your Father who speaks in you.
Matthew 10:20

For it is He who works in you to will and to do of His good pleasure
Philippians 2:13

OUR FIRST CAR

Christmas of 1954, Granny decided to buy a car. It was a 1948 Ford. She paid four hundred dollars for it. She borrowed some money from next year's work so we would have a way to get around. We were so grateful for this vehicle. Johnny didn't have a driver's license yet but he could drive. Now we wouldn't have to go to church on a wagon nor to town on the Bossman's truck. Johnny would drive to church and to the nearby stores. Granny got someone else to drive her into town. She told Johnny he had to get his license so he could take her to town. I just knew that it wasn't going to be hard for him to get his license, because he was a very smart young man. He failed the first time but he got it on the second try. We thought we could ride all around now, but Granny wasn't giving up that car to Johnny for his pleasure yet. He was to drive it when she wanted to go take care of her business.

Johnny was now 16 and was a respectable young man. He would always ask her if he could use the car and she always responded, "no, not now." Sometimes when Johnny drove Granny around he would ask to drive the car to his friend's house, but she would say no. He and his friend Clyde would walk or catch a ride to town so they could catch the train to Orangeburg to see a movie on the weekend. Johnny kept waiting patiently for the promises to come to pass for the use of the car. Occasionally on Wednesdays, when he wanted to go see his girlfriend, many times Lucille and I would comb Granny's hair so that she would fall asleep. Then we would help Johnny push the car from under the shed and push it down the road so he wouldn't have to walk to his girlfriend's house.

I really wanted my brother to have some pleasure. He was a very talented young man and very good with his hands. He would build toys for us out of wood and wire because Granny didn't believe in wasting money in toys. It was nothing for him to cut down pine trees and fashion wheels to put on the wagon and to make toy trucks. One person could ride in one of the little wagon at a time. He would even make his own toy tractors and cars from wire, and they looked so real. He made a wood and wire bus one time, and two little people could ride in it. Doing these things would keep his mind off the work that he had to do. God only knows what Johnny's life would have been like if only he had the chances. He had many talents and was a smart young man, but a good mind wasted. If he only had someone to work with his talents to give him a chance to be successful.

> *"The man who had received the five talents*
> *went at once and put his money to work and gained five more."*
> **St. Matthew 25:16**

Unfortunately, my brother did not have a chance. Brother was 17 and getting tired of the farm. Although he was now allowed to drive the car; he longed to get away. He wouldn't leave because he didn't want to break up our close-knit family. He was a tender-hearted person. Granny was 84 years old and her health was failing. She had to start seeing a doctor even though she didn't want to. You would never know she was feeling sick by her actions. We just noticed that her gate pace was slower than normal. We felt that she was hiding something from us. The thought of her being ill really hit home because we never knew her to be sick. We never heard her complain, not even of a headache. I suspected Granny wasn't feeling well because of the way she moved about and now Johnny started acting very strange and I felt like Johnny was in a worse condition than Granny.

I knew I needed to learn to drive. I talked to Granny about letting me drive the car up and down in the back yard but she always said, "don't touch that car." Contemplating Johnny leaving the farm, somebody needed to learn how to drive the car and I thought it should be me, but Granny said no. Johnny talked about going to live with our uncle in Philadelphia, so I didn't give up. I kept on asking Granny over and over to let me drive. She would say, "maybe later but definitely not now." I greatly respected and obeyed her, but the left side of my brain was telling me to crank up the car and pretend I was driving. I did that for a while. When she was tired from a long day's work, I would comb and scratch her hair until she fell asleep. Then I started the car and pull it up and down in the backyard until I got the feeling and movement of the car. One Saturday evening after Granny fell asleep, I decided it was time for me to check out my driving skills. I just knew I could drive so I cranked the car and backed it out of the yard into the road. I drove to the mailbox, which was about half of a mile from the house. As I was trying to turn the car around to get back home, the car got stuck in soft sand near the mailbox. I just knew I was in big trouble! However, the Curry family lived nearby and Mr. Curry saw the car was in trouble, so he came and rescued me. I thanked Mr. Curry repeatedly, but I knew I was in for a treat from Granny. I knew these old folks didn't keep anything from each other, especially when it concerned our well-being. I got the car back home safely, thank goodness! I didn't have any choice but to tell Granny and accept my punishment. If I didn't tell, Mr. Curry would have told her. Yes, I was chastened but after she saw my determination to drive, she allowed me to practice driving the car sometimes. So, I got my chance to openly drive. In addition, she allowed Johnny to continue to use the car for some of his recreational and Granny's outings.

PREPARING FOR LOVE

Although I was excited about being able to drive, I still lacked what the other girls my age had. I was not lucky like many young girls my age to have a nice living room set, a room for my company. Granny was not a person who worried about having expensive things. Our living room only contained a pot belly stove heater, a few sitting chairs, an old grand organ, and two small tables. I wanted a couch so badly. I would just imagine how one would look in the corner of our front room. I would try my decorating skills just to make our living room feel special and look its best. Granny would always tell me that she was going to get me a nice couch for the living room, but it never happened. I wanted a living room set so bad that my brother got me a back seat out of an old car and I cleaned it up. He helped me put it in the living room. We put three cinder blocks under each end and I covered it with my favorite colored bedspread which was blue. I pretended that I had a couch. I wanted Granny to feel good about letting me have company sometime and we would have somewhere nice to sit, especially if I could get a visit from a special gentleman named David Curry. I had a sho'nuff crush on him at that time. He was my first love. We had a cotton field courtship, but that's as far as it got. I had a couch in the front room but there was one more problem, I wanted the living room walls to look good too. Granny had her pride for the fields and I had my pride for her house, mainly for the front room.

I wanted to paint the walls but I didn't have any money to get the paint so I would wash the walls. Having the type of heating and cooking stove produced good food, good heat, and good smoke. I was that kind of girl who believed everything must be neat, clean and in its place. I was thinking about Granny's house. I want to make some changes to the front room. The well had just been cleaned out, and red clay was piled all on the side of the well.

When there is not a lot of money or resources, you use your imagination and ingenuity to come up with a wow factor. Just then God gave me an idea. I saw that clay and a piece of board and thought, "Humm, I wonder what it would look like to have a fresh coat of clay paint." so I decided to paint that piece of board and let it dry. Behold it was beautiful. I painted MY front room with a brush and a bucket of water and clay. I invested time for my room to look decent. My living room was a light pink and looking good.

Now our church would have gospel singing regularly on Sunday evening. Granny just loved Gospel singing, so we would go and enjoyed the Gospel program. Now I met this young man by the name of Cary, who was a gospel singer. There was something different and special about this young fellow. I didn't know what it was, but I did know he was very handsome. After meeting him several times at church, Granny and I fell in love with Cary (it was love at first site for me). She even saw him as a nice young man. She knew of his family. They all worked for the same man, but on different properties.

Ethel G. Wade

FAMILY TIES
CHAPTER THREE

A Blessing in the midst of two tragedies:

In 1956, Granny's pace was even slower, but it didn't affect her mind, she was still as sharp as a tack. As for my brother, he appeared to be sinking deeply in trouble. He couldn't keep his focus. Sometimes while working, he would pause at length, or stop altogether and just go to singing. Shy of scolding him, I'd tell him to go back to work so we could get the cotton hauled before the rain set in. He lost the motivation to pick two hundred pounds of cotton and lacked the focus to do a day's labor. I had to constantly prompt him to help get the cotton picked, but he kept singing, being in the safety of his own world; in that place where perhaps all his thoughts lived.

When he was little, Johnny seemed to be the professional worrier, but he's checked out of that hotel and now I'm the new owner. You see, my brother was all I had to help with Lucille, it felt a lot like swimming upstream in the most violent current. Granny said she believed his nerves went bad. I feared for him, feeling so helpless because I didn't know what to do.

One Wednesday night, Johnny went courting and stayed longer than usual. When he returned home, he was acting very strange, talking out of his head. It's like that date was the straw that broke the camel's back. Was it something she did or said? Johnny seemed delusional, saying, "I'm going to get married." I tried to calm him with my voice bidding him to come lay down, but he would not. I didn't want to alarm Granny, knowing she wasn't in her best way, but the alarm sounded for her grandson, and she responded with her prayers. Johnny was finally persuaded to come inside so Granny would continue in prayer and encouragement for him that everything was going to be alright. She assured him he'd see the doctor first thing daybreak. So, he laid down and went to sleep. As for me, I got absolutely no sleep at all. I just tossed and turned all night. When morning arrived, I knew that we had to get him to a doctor. He said some funny feeling was running up and down in his legs. I went next door to Mr. Row and asked him if he would take my sick brother to the doctor for Granny. Mr. Row and his family lived next door to us on the farm and they had their own vehicle. They were kind-hearted people and Mr. Row was like a father to Johnny. He said, "Yes, I'll take him." I wanted to be there for my brother at the doctor's but I was best served being with Granny and Lucille. Mr. Row and one of Johnny's co-workers started to the doctor. When they returned home, they both looked so troubled. I studied their eyes and body language and I knew something had gone terribly wrong. Mr. Row gave me a prescription for Johnny and told us the bad news. The doctor said my brother was on the verge of a nervous breakdown and the medicine was to help him rest. Brother would just cry and cry and make me cry. I thought on how hard he worked in his short life and how he was so mistreated on that old job. Now he has legitimate complaints of strange feelings traveling in his legs and acting bizarre. Everything Johnny and I went through was traveling cross-country in my mind. He asked me to rub his legs. I rubbed them with alcohol two or three times a night and prayed he would be well. The only real break I got was when he would take his medicine and go to sleep. My world was turned upside down. My friend Cary would come by and check on us from time to time when in our area. Talking to him brought me some normalcy and comfort. Cary was a God sent. He would comfort Johnny and do what he could for him because he knew what he had gone through on the job.

I would also remember what my Granny would say, "No matter what happens in your life, you're never alone. The Lord will never leave you nor forsake you." Our neighbors found out about Johnny's problem and mentioned us in their prayers. That gave me hope. Sometimes I felt I couldn't go on. It felt as if the whole world was on my shoulders. I continually asked the Lord to help my brother and thanked Him for any miracle or restoration. Now Granny and Johnny were sick! Our cousin Junior Singleton from Norway would come sometimes and help me feed the livestock and see after everything else I was unable to do.

Sometimes Cousin Junior would stay overnight and talk with Johnny which gave me relief. I remember this as if it were this morning; on the afternoon of the second Friday in September of 1956, Johnny left with the car, which was inconceivable, without Granny's blessing. Due to his legs, he was in no condition to drive alone. What was going to happen to him? All I wanted was for Johnny to return home safely with that car. Granny didn't know at this point, so if Johnny hurried back, she'd never have to know. When it got dark and Johnny was not home, I know I had to tell Granny. Lucille and I waited practically all night for Johnny to return but he didn't. When Saturday morning came and he had not returned, I had this strange feeling that something awful had happened to our brother. I could feel it. I went on and prepared breakfast because Granny needed to eat. We waited and waited. We were all hurting.

I told Granny that Johnny must have been sick to do something like this. Granny told me to ask Mr. Row if he would take her to town to see if anyone had heard or seen anything of her grandson. Just as I was about to leave the house, a man that worked with Johnny drove up. He informed us that Johnny was picked up by a highway patrolman on the night before, around six o'clock. He heard they took him to the hospital in Orangeburg so that he could get help. However, it would be 30 days before we could see him. We found out Johnny went to a girlfriend's house in Norway, but we never heard anything from her in regards to his behavior.

Just before the 30 days were up, a man came to the house from Orangeburg saying they took Johnny to Crafts Farrow Mental Hospital in Columbia, South Carolina.

Now, we knew that our brother had a nervous breakdown and his condition was serious. I was hoping my poor brother would not have to be in that hospital long. I cried myself to sleep many nights thinking about him. I would say, "Lord please don't leave me now with Granny and Johnny sick, and Lucille with her condition." Lucille always tried to comfort me when she saw that I was troubled. She was there doing whatever she could. She was always a blessing in her own way. To God be the glory.

In October 1956, Granny wasn't doing well and we were still hoping to see Johnny. During this time, Cary and I had been dating about nine months. Cary seemed to have a vested interest in what I was going through physically, mentally, and emotional. Ray Charles could see that all hell was breaking loose in my family and Cary's compassion kept him coming just for me. I felt deeply inside that Cary wanted to help with the work load. He saw how I was trying to finish gathering the crops, caring for the livestock, watching out for Granny and Lucille, and anticipating seeing my brother on October 21, 1956. God gave him a burden for my heart and He saw and understood everything.

MARRIAGE
CHAPTER FOUR

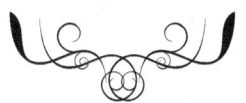

Cary and I courted at church and my home. We had serious conversations about Johnny and the mistreatment on the job. Johnny was taken advantage of because of his humility. He was highly intelligent and a man of few words. The whites didn't know how else to break him except to misuse him. His humility was mistaken for weakness, so they took full advantage and sported him. It made me angry to hear what happened, we knew very little about his work conditions. Cary told me Bossman's overseers had a field day with Johnny over lining up fences. He had such a skill and precision that when the fence was completed, it looked like a military gate lined up. Johnny's co-workers would speak on his behalf saying the fence was lined up beautifully, but the hecklers would make him do again and again. He reminded me of Christ when Christ didn't say a word on his behalf, but was mocked and was jeered.

He was oppressed, and he was afflicted, yet he opened not his mouth: he is brought as a lamb to the slaughter, and as a sheep before her shearers is dumb, so he openeth not his mouth.
Isaiah 53:7

Now dealing with my brother's mental condition, Cary realized it was a lot on me. I recall one Wednesday night early in October of 1956, Cary asked for my hand in marriage. I didn't know what to say, I was shocked! I hoped one day I would become a wife, but I wasn't thinking about marriage right then. I was more interested in his motive. I didn't need pity. I believed it was love at first sight when we met that Sunday afternoon at the gospel singing at Church. However, I needed to make sure he loved me for me and was not just feeling sorry for me. I desperately needed to hear those three powerful words, but I just needed to know if he meant it. He answered, "I want to marry you, not because I feel sorry for you. I want to marry you because I love you and want to be with you to help you through whatever you're dealing with." I thought, OOH but inside I was screaming "Yes, Yes, Yes!" God lifted a burden from me. I had no idea that God would tell my business to Granny before we could get the thought out. Cary with his gentle voice said, "Now let's go and talk to your Grand momma!" Just as Cary and I walked into Granny's room and before he could ask her, she very slowly said "Yes, Cary, you can have her in marriage. I was praying you two would get married and God has answered my prayer."

Granny, with her wisdom from God, said, "Now Mae, I want you to know, you and Cary seem to love one another. Cary, you must continue to love her. Mae, know that your husband will be the head, and you must always respect your husband standing by his side. Cary, if she gets out of order, you know what to do (but not like Harpo). If you two stick together, you will have a good long married life. I have sent up many prayers for you all and I want you both to know something before you get married…teeth and tongue will fall out sometime and you will bite your tongue sometimes but they stay in your mouth together as a married couple."

Granny's words have lived within me up to this day. She will never be forgotten and we still remember her words today.

She also said, "Dear ones remember, everything is not going to be sugar and spice and everything nice, always remember you will have your share of ups and downs... Know that man will put you down, but the Lord will pick you up, and He will stand by both of you when the going gets tough... and never believe everything you hear until it is proven and believe only half of what your eyes see because your own eyes can fool you. Don't forget to pray. Pray for your enemies as well as your friends. Know that prayer is the key to the Kingdom and faith will unlocks the door to His heart; *which is righteous, peace and joy in the Holy Ghost* Romans **14:17**.

On October 13, 1956, Cary and I were united in holy matrimony at the courthouse in Orangeburg, S.C. Probate Judge J. M. Hughes married us. It was one of the happiest days of my life. I knew in my heart Cary was my soul mate. We got married on his 19th birthday, so that made our wedding day extra special. My 16th birthday was not quite a month away. Now I had a husband to help, comfort, and care for me through these troubled times. He was such a blessing in every way. He helped me finish gathering the crops, we got some help with the cotton and we took care of the rest of the farm work. Granny was so weak by now and could barely get out of bed, she was 85. I didn't realize she had colon cancer and there was nothing the doctors could do. She would ask about her grandson, Johnny, I assured her he would be alright because he was getting treatment.

Thirty days was up and I made it to the next biggest day of my life, the day I would lay eyes on my brother Johnny. On Sunday, October 21, 1956, my husband and I left for Columbia, while my aunt Ollie Grant sat with Lucille and Granny. Ollie was Granny's baby girl from her first husband, Oliver. Cary and I had very little to say. I suppose each of us was thinking and praying in anticipation. I was hoping and praying Johnny would be in a good mood so we could converse. I expected to see a melancholy man balled up like a bag of bones in bed. However, when I got to the desk, I was astonished when the receptionist and nurse told us Johnny would visit us in the waiting room. "WHAT?" I was truly amazed. We waited anxiously for him to walk through those doors. I just wanted to see him. When he crossed the threshold to where we were, it was a feeling that will never be erased. There he was. I will never forget that look on his face. It was a look of joy! I felt like I could fly from the overwhelming thrill in my heart! We clutched each other in a hug and didn't want to let go. Although I didn't want him to see me cry, I couldn't help myself. I wept happy tears. My brother seemed to be in a good state of mind. Those 31 days seemed like 31 years.

After our greeting, Cary told him that he had married his sister. Johnny's face lit up and he responded with, "Cary, you are my brother-in-law?" He grabbed Cary and they embraced. When they did turn loose, he said, "I am glad you and Mae got married." Johnny didn't act like someone who had a mental problem. He was in his good mind, with a clean shaved head and he seemed as if nothing was wrong. He looked well. We sat down and started to talk. We had dinner on the outside with him so we could relax and enjoy our time together with him. He started continuously asking about Granny. He wanted to know how she was doing and I told him she was doing well for her age. I didn't tell him she was confined to the bed because I didn't want to cause him worry. It was best for him not to know her condition.

I told him Granny was worried and concerned about him, but we diverted his attention from Granny. We asked him if he wanted to tell us what really happened to him on that Friday afternoon when he left home. He told us that he had gone to town and stopped by the café and stayed there for a while. Then he said he left the café and headed out of town towards Orangeburg. Just as he got out of the city limits, he said a highway patrolman stopped him. The patrolman told him to get out of the car and he said he did as he was told. The patrolman grabbed his hands and started to put handcuffs around his wrists. He said he asked the patrolman what he did but the patrolman didn't answer him. He just ordered him to get in the car and didn't say a word. The patrolman took him to Orangeburg jail and put him in a very dark room at the Jail house. He said it was so dark he could not see his hands in front of him. He said he just cried. All I could say was, "O my Lord." My brother was already on the verge of having a nervous breakdown, and they didn't know by putting him in a dark room just made him sicker. He said he didn't know how long he spent in that dark jail cell... only God knew. I asked him if he could remember anything that he might have done to make the patrolman stop him. He said Mae, "the only thing I can think of was maybe I didn't use my hand signal because I wasn't feeling good."

After listening to Johnny tell us what happened to him, I was brokenhearted and really at a loss for words. All I could think of was my poor brother. A hard working, intelligent and humble young person suffered so much because people lacked the knowledge concerning his condition. If that policemen had only known he was on the verge of having a nervous breakdown, they could have gotten the right help.

Surely, Johnny wanted to come home with us, but we knew he couldn't. He didn't want us to leave him, and it was so hard for us leave him. On the way home, there was great relief in my soul seeing my brother walking and talking, but still so many questions and no answers. Cary and I returned home. Granny was a sick woman, but when we told her about Johnny's condition, she smiled and thanked the Lord. She was such an independent woman but life and illness caused her to be unable to get up or move around on her own, but still, she praised God and continued to instill the Word in us.

Granny called Aunt Ollie, Lucille, my husband, and me around her bedside to talk to us. She spoke in a very low tone, but she had found the strength to tell us to stick together. She said, "no matter what problems might occur in your life, just trust the Lord and He will see you through." She added, "Cary, you and Mae promise me that you will stand by Lucille and Johnny. I'm going to leave you all, but you are going to be alright." Our Granny Rosetta Grant Ross expired the night of November 22, 1956 at 85 years old.

The year of 1956 involved hardship and blessings. My brother suffered from mental illness on September 25, 1956. Cary and I were married on October 13, 1956, and Granny left us on November 22, 1956.

The loss of my Granny was a time of sadness, joy, and heartache all wrapped into one emotional package, nevertheless I just knew I had to have the strength for my brother and my sister. I just thanked God that I didn't have to face it alone. He sent me a husband to be with me every step of the way. As we prepared for Granny's service, we found out that her insurance had lapsed. When she took sick, the insurance man stopped coming to pick up her monthly payments. The last time he came by, he saw that Granny wasn't doing well. We tried our best to contact him to give him the money with no luck. I went to his house and left notes many times concerning Granny's insurance, but we never heard from him again. She maintained her policy prior to us coming to live with her; she may have neglected other things, she paid that policy. I found out that she was not on record at the insurance company. They came, took the money, and pocketed it. That really hit where it hurt the most.

Thank God for her three children out of ten that were

still alive and well; two daughters and one son. They got together and put her away, with a little help from her boss who was supposed to be holding Granny's money. However, he told us he wasn't holding any money for her, but he would give us two hundred dollars to help with her burial. I had to borrow ten dollars so that Lucille and I could get a pair of gloves and stockings.

After all of Granny's hard work over the years, we still faced a hardship trying to bury her. After six years of hard work on this farm, we had nothing.

Granny would tell us the reason we had to work so hard was so she would have some type of inheritance after she was gone but it didn't work out that way. It was just hard work and nothing to show for it. Only heartaches and pain, sunshine and rain, but God sees and knows all about it.

For mine eyes are upon all their ways: they are not hid from my face, neither is their iniquity hid from mine eyes.
Jeremiah 16:17

With Granny gone, no inheritance, no burial, I need to sell the livestock to help support my sister. I prayed continually for my sister to get help because I didn't want my husband to feel obligated for her care. He was making only $2.50 a day, which was $12.50 a week. That was all he made for a while, and we had to make do. I just couldn't let my sister down. We promised Granny that we would look out for her and Johnny, so I did all I could to help my husband. I thanked God that I was taught how to work for what I needed.

We sold the mule and the cow to get the money needed to help my sister. We didn't even receive our troubles worth, but the little money rendered was a help for her. Getting rid of Lottie, the mule and Bettie the cow was a big relief to me because I no longer had to cut corn tops, or strip corn leaves to feed them. We had a little corn left to feed our few hogs and chickens. As I faced tough times with my sister, I remembered the many good neighboring families that stood by us on that farm with Granny. These families and their children were a blessing to us. We visited as often as we could. They were as concerned about us as we were about them. I just thank God for them and their children still today.

Suddenly, I was punched in the face with reality. Here I was, a 16 years old newlywed, with responsibility of taking care of my intellectually challenged, 17-year-old sister. I also had to keep in touch with my 18-year-old brother, who lived in a mental hospital, while learning to provide for myself. However, I remember what Granny used to say, "together with the Lord, you all can make it."

Although my sister was there, I had many days when I felt lonely while my husband was at work. Lucille talked very little. Sometimes she would say, "Mae, I'm here with you." I would try my best not to cry when she was around me, but it was impossible to hide it from her sometime. Lucille would comfort me and let me know that she was there for me.

Christmas was near and I needed to visit Johnny again. We hadn't informed him that our Granny had passed. I didn't know how he was going to take it but I had to tell him. We went to see him the weekend before Christmas and we found him doing well. The first thing he wanted to know was how Granny was doing. I managed to tell him that she had expired. I was more anxious about telling Johnny but to my surprise he took the news well. He said, "Mae, Granny was old and she was a hardworking woman. The Lord knew she needed some rest." His response made me wonder why he was still in the hospital. I knew Johnny had been through a lot of pain, but I just thanked God for the strength He gave Johnny to endure.

My brother had to go through some things, being in the hospital, but his time there helped him grown by leaps and bounds. He didn't seem to let anything bother him too much and that was good for his overall mental health and stability.

Ethel G. Wade

MY THREE AUNTS
CHAPTER FIVE

Cary's Family Helping

Cary and I continued living in the house where Granny died for three months but February 1957, we decided to move near Cary's parents, close to Norway. His parents lived on the same Bossman's property, but a different location. I was more than thrilled leave the Fillmore place because I had so many bad memories. We would reside near Cary's parents and other family members. They lived in a big community. As in-laws, they were good to Lucille and me, especially, Cary's three aunts. Aunt Mary and Aunt Meter Mae had children close to Lucille and my age, but Aunt Annie Lee didn't have any of her own, so everybody's children were her children. She had one adopted son and who could imagine that my sister would find herself a member of Aunt Annie Lee's family.

Lucille was 17 and the boys were looking. I was newly married at 16, so Cary's precious aunt relieved us and took Lucille as her very own. Cary and I could now practice being married without the burdens of family responsibility. These three women opened the doors of their homes to my sister and me. I could plainly see my sister coming out of her shell, especially when it was babysitting time. She loved to babysit for her aunt's children. They would let her spend the night sometime with their daughters. The help I received from my aunts was such a blessing and help to me. They helped to lift a weight off my shoulders so I could be a married young woman.

> *O the chief Musician, A Psalm of David. Blessed is he that considereth the poor: the LORD will deliver him in time of trouble.*
> **Psalm 46:1**

Now I was about 18 miles away from my church and closer to Cary's church. Our church services were at the same time on first and third Sundays. I was a bench warmer but Cary sang on the choir. I saw a conflict between my husband and me brewing, but then I remembered what Granny taught me. She said, "Mae, you're the woman and Cary is the man. He is your head and you are to stand by his side. If you ever see a problem happening in your marriage, you should do something about it right away. Do it for peace in your marriage and don't wait." Attending two churches caused a problem which bought me to another truth my Granny said, **"A stitch in time, saves nine stitches."** She was saying don't let the problem get too big before you do something about it. In essence, she was telling me to talk things out. Keep the line of communication open at all times and recognize my own short comings. Lastly, work together toward a common goal." He and I talked things over, and I joined his church. I didn't want any extra obstacles in our life. Going to one church also made it possible for me to go and see my brother more often.

MASSIVE STRUGGLE
CHAPTER SIX

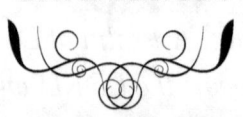

In 1957, I became pregnant with our first child. We were ecstatic to be new parents. All I could think of was I'm having my very own little person to love and care for. I prayed day and night that my baby would be well and healthy. I had been through so much with my sister and brother's challenges.

I needed to know more about my heritage on both sides. Now that I was having my own child, I was curious about my family history. Finding out about Daddy's brother, Uncle Earnest could shed light on the family. Previously, we would converse by phone. He came to visit with Granny a few times, but now our correspondence was only by mail. He hadn't met Cary yet.

By May of 1957, time was getting close for my first child to be born. Nonetheless, I was still doing a little work with my in-laws on the farm, picking cotton. I was doing whatever I could to help Cary with my sister. She was not receiving any kind of financial assistance yet, and we were surviving on one income, with a baby on the way. In the meantime, I was still trying to get help for Lucille. I would often recall things that Granny said, like,

"Mae, it's going to be times in your life when you will have hard bones to chew, and bitter pills to swallow." I was being told, by some, to put my sister in an institutional home. I could truly say that this was one of those trying times.

It was time for my first child to be born. Everybody was excited. Lucille was so happy that she was going to be an auntie. Our blessing arrived on Sunday, June 2, 1957. Our first-born child was a little girl. She weighed 7.5 pounds. She was the most beautiful little baby girl I had ever seen. Her little face was so full and round. Cary and I were so happy and grateful for her. Cary named her Zener, after one of his brother's friends.

We were still living near Cary's parents on the Huffman place. Cary was working even harder now trying to make ends meet. I nursed my baby so we didn't have to buy milk. Now he said his Bossman was talking about giving him a little raise. He continued to work in hopes of Cary getting a raise, but it was only talk.

We needed more income, it was necessary for our little one who was growing so fast. Lucille was good with Zener but I wasn't comfortable enough to leave her with Zener alone, so often I would take the baby to Aunt Annie Lee's house. Lucille babysat Zener and Aunt Annie Lee babysat Lucille. On the weekends, Cary would take Lucille, Zener, and me to see Johnny. We got to spend time as a family with Johnny as regularly as possible. Johnny was a new uncle and Lucille thought she was momma too. They loved our new edition. Johnny's spirit was lifted each time he would see the baby. We tried to spend as much as we could with Johnny.

Time passed and we were now expecting our second child. I gave birth to a handsome son on December 6, 1958. We named him Cary Jr. He weighed nine pounds and they were so precious to look at, better than watching TV. Now we were blessed with a son and a daughter. We saw ourselves in those little bodies.

Now with a second child, we anticipated better financial conditions, but Cary were still the same $2.50 a day. I knew my husband deserved a better paying job but I remembered the words of my old Granny, "In life, you will have to crawl before you walk." I tried to keep that in mind because I felt like we were surely crawling, sometimes crawling twice.

After more than two years, it finally happened, the state approved financial assistance for Lucille. It had been a long time coming, but the wait was well worth it. We were so pleased to be receiving a small monthly check for $27. Things were looking up.

A few months later, Cary came home with some good news. Cary said Bossman was going to build a milk dairy and wanted him to help get it started, which meant more money. Thank goodness! Unfortunately, this meant having to move closer to the dairy. The house near to the dairy wasn't finished yet, but Bossman wanted us to move right away. He had another house for us to move in, but he knew Cary didn't want to move his family in the middle of nowhere surrounded by woods and fields where grain was planted for cattle. Cary took the house temporarily, which we told would be about three months at the most.

I was afraid to move away from Cary's parents since they were such good help with our babies. His aunt Annie Lee would come over and keep our little ones, and look out for my sister sometimes. Her help was invaluable because it would allow me to do a little domestic work and provide assistance to my husband. I would help our boss lady two half days a week, ironing and cleaning her home. I made $4.00 a week which allowed me to get some little things needed for the house. My time away from home posed a major problem for Lucille. She was nineteen and some boys tried to take advantage of her. We didn't have neighbors living close by because we sat smack dab in the middle of a field, surround by the woods, and cows grazing. Some of the boys were at the height of disrespect and total disregard toward my sister. A young fellow whom attended the same church fellowship as we did was one of the head culprits in messing with Lucille. We knew each other's family, so he well understood Lucille's vulnerability. Lucille told what was going on and I stepped in like a superhero and spoke up for her. I spoke from John 3:16 when I told him that God didn't make all of us alike and we all are created by Him and He loves us all the same."

Although I didn't like living in the middle of a field of cows away from civilization, one positive advantage was our abundant garden. We had the best garden spot ever. We could have won every garden growing contest and could've been featured in any garden magazine, because it grew vegetables like crazy like I've never seen before. We knew it was the cows that gave us their choice blessings. Another advantage was Cary bringing milk from the dairy farm that yielded butter.

By mid-December 1959, I started feeling overwhelmed dealing with high growing cow food and direct sun and heat. Bossman, with all his lies enticed my family away from our good home. I was morbid and depressed most days. I was ready to leave!

I did not want Lucille to see me this way, so I would walk to the edge of the woods and sit on a log and cry out to God. The corn and millet had grown so tall; it hid the house. I prayed and asked God to get us out of this situation. Carry got tired of asking Bossman when the house be completed, but I kept on pushing him to remain persistent. However, Bossman turned a deaf ear to my husband, Cary.

July 1960, I was about to deliver our third child. I was under much duress and sick most of the time. Lucille was my right hand since there was little work I could do. She was there for me, doing what she could. There had been no consideration in finishing the house. Cary was now working two jobs, one at the dairy farm and the other at the Bossman's auto mechanic shop after hours. When Cary got off work from the first job, he and his brother would go to the second job and work from 6:00 pm until.

August 7, 1960, Curtis was born. Cary Jr has a little brother. Our second precious little boy weighed 8.5 lbs. After giving birth to Curtis, I began hemorrhaging. The mid-wife thought she was going to lose me, but the Lord revived me. I was under so much pressure with all I was undergoing. My body was so weak. I did recover by the help of God and was strong enough to take Zener, Cary Jr., and our new addition Curtis to visit my brother at the hospital. Brother had a sad look because he was unable to come home with us. Leaving was always hard but seeing the children would lift his spirits. Johnny would say, "Mae, I hope to be home soon so I can find myself a wife and have some children of my own."

It got to the point, I felt Johnny seeing the children caused him sadness and worry, so we brought them less. I didn't want to hurt him. However, his doctor said he was doing much better, and I kept on praying for him.

Lucille would ask when would her brother come home. It was rough. Although I had my own family now, we missed having him around, and anticipated his soon return.

One summer day in 1961, Johnny was able to make a home visit. This felt like Thanksgiving and Christmas. Everyone was ecstatic. The food was smelling, the children laughed and played with him. It was a house filled with joy. While watching the happiness of the room, I reflected on the ages of my children, and realized that Zener was about one year older than me when I lost my father. Cary Jr. was three, Curtis was one, and now walking. It brought back the memories of my parents being snatched away at an early age. I prayed that I could see my children live in their old age. I started sharing with my little ones early, some of the good things that Granny taught me. One thing she taught was the purpose of sharing and caring for one another. She'd say, "Love one another and share with your brother and your sister." Another valuable lesson was, "Don't ever look down on someone less fortunate than you, unless you look down to pick them up." I could never forget her teachings.

Uncle Ernest and the Promise

I was so thankful that Uncle Ernest continued to keep in touch with us. As promised, he was going to send for Lucille and let her spend some times with he and his family. He was the only living brother of my father. By all accounts, I did whatever it took to keep the lines of communication open. The next letter we received from Uncle was November of 1961, it said for us to expect Lucille's ticket in the mail in a few days. Lucille was so excited to know that she was going to the big city of Philadelphia, PA. I was so happy for her, but I knew I was going to miss her help. The children had grown so attached to her, but I knew Lucille needed a change. We received her ticket and I got her ready for the trip. Lucille was traveling by train so I had to tag her since her speech was not clear. She left from Denmark, South Carolina. As I watched that train pull off, all I could do was hold back my tears. This was the first time my sister and I were ever separated. I felt as if a part of me was leaving my own body as my sister boarded the train. The next day Lucille arrived in Philadelphia safely.

Cary and I now had the chance to experience parenthood alone. Uncle kept us informed on how Lucille was adjusting to the surrounding. She was smitten with the family up north and with what she saw of the city. This was a great consolation, however a difficult sacrifice. Lucille has always been with me through life, marriage, and our children, but the benefits for her to enjoy life in another environment was a sacrifice I was willing to make.

We attended church regularly because Cary was a gospel singer, and a choir member. I ushered at times when I had help with my babies. We were in church practically every weekend. I needed that spiritual connection to keep me going. Now pregnant with our fourth child, the house still was not finished. I was hoping that I wouldn't have to give birth to another child in this environment. Cary kept asking Bossman when was he going to have the house ready. "Soon," he'd say, but three months turned into almost three years.

In the Spring of 1962, things got worse around the house. The millet had grown so tall that Bossman decided to let the cows eat straight from the field instead of cutting them down. Two feet tall electric fencing was installed to keep the cows from invading our home. Like a lady lifting her long dress to protect her fall, the cows seemed to tiptoe through the tulips, over the wire and straight to our abode where the cows did their business for us to smell and step in. It seemed on purpose more than laziness, but the result was still the same. They ate from my garden. I had to clean manure from my steps before I could take my babies to and from the car. Who could phantom such treatment of any human being to live in such inhumane conditions? Bossman was telling Cary one thing and doing another.

By August 1962, school was opening and our little girl was old enough to attend. The joy of a mother and child preparing for a new experience was ours. It was a great feeling to get her ready for her first day of school. From fixing her hair, lining out her clothes, helping her put them on, having breakfast together for her very first day of school, to walking her to the road for the bus. This was just so exciting for her and me. However, moving about through all the mess of manure, mullet and field was its own painstaking task and journey. Regardless, I continued to expect better days.

With Zener in school, I spent much of my days gathering the garden and tending to the other children, until it was time to meet her from the bus. I got a stronger job; that job was canning. Every year since Granny taught me, I would jar all I could get my hands on from the big garden. More than a hundred quarts of fruits and vegetables like peaches, pears and peppers would go in the canning jars. You name it, and I canned it. Building from my frustration of being in this surrounding mess, I'm sure that was the culprit to jar up everything. Everything was multiplying. It was a blessing and a curse. I figured it out much later that the cows were eating and dropping, and I was stepping, shaking, picking and canning.

Cary was still working two jobs, receiving slightly under a $100 a week. We were a family of five expecting number six. It wasn't easy. I cried many days and nights about our plight. By day, I sat on my prayer log by the edge of the woods and cried out to God and by night I would lie and cry briny tears silently on my pillow. Although it took Cary a long time to realize he was lied to and needed to find another job, God helped him to step out of his denial.

On October 14, 1962 I gave birth to our fourth child, a handsome, 7.5 pound baby boy. We named him Rodney. We were definitely a family of six. My husband had been seeking better jobs, but they were hard to come by. I believed God for a way out of this environment.

THE HOUSE BURNING:
About three weeks after Rodney's birth, I got up early that Friday morning feeling great. I remember it as if it

were yesterday! I felt like cleaning. Having a baby has its joys and its restrictions. Watching my children was better than watching TV, and so much of the time was spent doing just that. I didn't have much time for organizing the house and cleaning. However, on this day I gutted old papers and mail, washed clothes, and made dinner for my family. Cary and I would generally have dinner together around one o'clock in the afternoon, then he'd return to work. Laziness didn't come on me at all that day, and after he left, I continued to clean. I tried to have my work completed by the time I would get Zener from school. Cary Jr. and Curtis were playing in the back room. I nursed the baby and put him down for a nap.

When Zener arrived, all the children sat for snacks in our huge kitchen. I loved the way this well-built house was framed. It had three huge bedrooms, front room, dining area, and front and back porches. Each bedroom and the front room had a fireplace. One bedroom was used for canned foods. I had many shelves filled with my food from the big garden. The second bedroom was for the children, and the third bedroom was for me and Cary.

I picked up with the cleaning. I moved boxes and bags that were filled with scraps from the sewing done for others and myself. I put in scraps from the sewing and old paper I no longer needed in the fireplace. When suddenly, I heard a crackling and popping noise. I went to the room where the children were playing, but the noise was not coming from there. I proceeded to the kitchen and

everything was okay there, but when I got to the living room, the crackling got louder. I looked around the room but didn't see anything until I looked up. I thought I saw a great light shining through that old wooden loft. It was a peculiar site I'd never seen before. I thought perhaps it was the sunlight, but the sun had already set in the tree tops. I went outside to wrap my mind around what was really going on, hoping for a different result, I looked up and behold, there it was, the house was on fire. I started screaming and hollering for help, but I knew I couldn't be heard way back up in all these woods and mullet and fields. I ran back inside to get my children from the flaming top house. I took my baby in my arms and made sure my three oldest were right behind me. I started to run toward the dairy house where Cary worked, frantically trying to get someone's attention for that old burning house. I kept my eyes on my little ones. they were all crying and confused; not knowing what was going on. Little Curtis had lost his shoes, but they were all following me. I looked back at the house and I could see half of the rooftop engulfed in flames and smoke. The dairy was about a quarter of a mile
from the house. When I finally reached the entrance, Cary and his brother heard my great panic and hysteria. They ran out and saw the smoke and fire.

The top of the house was completely engulfed in flames. We picked up our babies one by one and headed back towards the house. When we got there, the living room loft was in the color of amber. The ceiling was about to collapse. Cary and his brother, Matthew, risked their lives in every effort to save something from the burning inferno. Matthew managed to pick up an innerspring mattress and drug it out of the first bedroom.

Cary ran for our clothes closet and put his arms around all the clothes he could hold. He managed to salvage a large arm full of clothes because I hung them all in one direction, the way my 4-H club instructor at school taught. It is good to listen to those who gives even the simplest lessons. Granny taught us that teachers were our parents away from home. Imagine a simple lesson of hanging all hangers in the same direction saving clothes and lives.

With literally seconds to escape, Cary and Matthew barely avoided the loft in the front room caving in on them. The Lord heard my prayers and blessed them to get out safety.

My prayers were to be delivered from those living conditions, and the burning of that house was God's way of answering my prayers. I will miss the big rooms and the best garden ever, but GOD is a prayer answering God and an on time deliverer. It was a time in my life I will never forget. We all were blessed to be alive. We lost everything except a mattress and a few clothes, but nothing was broken or missing in our spirits, bodies, or minds. I was sad that we lost all Granny's valuables, but nothing was lost concerning her impression in my heart; it will last forever. I had my many memories of Granny, and all of my good times outweighed the bad times. She will never die as long as I live. God be praised.

My husband's uncle Carlie and his family ministered comfort to us by giving us shelter that same Friday evening until the first of the week. In this time of trouble, people came and showed their kindness. Even the wolves among the sheep came bearing their guilty gifts. I couldn't believe what I was seeing, furniture and clothing, if you could name it, we got it. Many of the things we got were very good, including a nice three door top oven stove.

Nothing could replace Granny's things, like her old two door stove, four-ten shotgun, which folded up small enough to put it in your pocket, her old corn Sheller, her old hand butter churner, and other old sentimental things. However, we were grateful for what we received, like a sewing machine so I could continue to make clothes. Granny's things meant so much and I was devastated at the loss.

EVERYTHING GONE! It was all gone. All the vegetables and fruits I spent so much of my time canning that year was LOST. All I could see and hear was rumbling, snapping, crackling, and popping. The ammunition in that old four-ten shotgun going off, and the canning jars were cracking, popping and cooking. God knew what he was doing to get us from that awful way of living, but Lord, what a tradeoff. However, we were thankful we escaped with our very lives.

Hard to believe I stayed in a house for almost three years, based on a three-month promissory note of lies. Three working days after losing almost everything, Bossman said the house he originally promised us was NOW finished. WHAT? I was flabbergasted and completely in utter DISBELIEF. Wednesday of the next week, we, like little lost children, moved from Uncle Carlie's home to the house that was promised to us more than three years before. I was trying to be happy in this house, but happiness was the farthest thing from my mind. I was hurting and I was stone angry. If ever there was a time to leave this master-slave, mind-gaming, and mental whoredom, the time was NOW! I was ready! My anger was so great until there were days, I contemplated Bossman's own judgment at my hand, but I remembered what the Scriptures said:

"To me belongeth vengeance, and recompence; their foot shall slide in due time: for the day of their calamity is at hand, and the things that shall come upon them make haste."
Deuteronomy 32: 35

"Dearly beloved, avenge not yourselves, but rather give place unto wrath: for it is written, Vengeance is mine; I will repay, saith the Lord."
Romans 12:19

I had to pray to keep myself together and not flatten old Bossman's place like a shopping mall parking lot. As a consolation prize, Cary got a small raise which helped a lot, but there was still no happiness. Bad memories constantly rehearsed themselves in my mind, like a choir of bad singing; from my brother's mental sickness, the shifting, the moving, the deaths, to now. My husband and I talked night after night, trying to find solace and peace, but there was none. We were hurt, almost beyond repair. Anywhere else would be better than where we were.

The finished house had three bedrooms a large kitchen, living room, and a bathroom inside for the first time. However, the pain outweighed the joys of having these well-deserved amenities.

Sister Return Saved My Life

It was January of 1963, Lucille returned home after living with our uncle and his family for a year. We were so happy for her to be back. She was looking good. She left home weighing more than 180 pounds, wearing a size 18, but she came back a size 10! She transformed into another person. Her hair was dark and lovely, bone straight down to her shoulders. It was unbelievable how she changed in one year. My uncle and family supplied Lucille with clothes which was good considering her clothes perished in the fire. Uncle also sent boxes of clothes for our children and that blessed us.

The children were overjoyed to see their aunt back home. Our daughter Zener was six years old, Cary Jr. was four years old, Curtis was two years old, and our baby Rodney was about eight weeks old. Lucille was so happy to be back around her niece and nephews. My children were at the age where they could really enjoy her. They couldn't keep their eyes off her. It was like none of them had seen her before. She was so good with them. After getting settled, we took off to the hospital to see Johnny. He was so happy to see everyone, especially his sister, Lucille. He was amazed to see how great she looked. He wanted to know everything about the city. He was so excited as she tried to explain her visit to him. He would say when he got out of the hospital he wanted to go to the city and visit Uncle Earnest and his family. I was hoping the same for him.

About mid-July of 1963, I woke up that morning not feeling my best. I hadn't been feeling well for a while, but I kept going. I found out I was pregnant again with baby number five. Our youngest Rodney was only eight months old, so being pregnant again was NOT welcomed news. Later that morning, Cary Jr. and Curtis were up and playing in the hall. I went to the bathroom and closed the door. I sat down and suddenly, I felt really hot and faint. I opened the door trying to get some air. I felt sensations I had never felt before.

The last thing I remembered was the feeling of something cold being shoved down my throat. I felt as if I was choking. Immediately, my little hall alarms went off. My beautiful sons were the alarm system that yelled, "Mommy! Mommy," and that sent a shock wave through the air.

The sound of their voices resounded to the point that my sister awoke to their panic. Lucille heard the boys yelling, and my she found me passed out on the floor. She tried to arouse me, get me up, but could not, so she ran to the dairy for help. Cary came. I didn't remember anything after I felt that coolness in my throat. When I came to, I saw Cary on one side and my sister on the other. I noticed my restrictions. I had all of these tubes attached to me. I was in the hospital. Then all my feelings left about me and my focus immediately went straight for my unborn baby and his condition. Cary relayed the news, I had lost the baby but I was going to be alright according to the doctor. Cary said it was a close call.

The doctor said if Cary had gotten me to the hospital one moment later than, I might not have survived. He explained my condition as being gas and indigestion. Something so simple as gas and indigestion almost cost me life. I knew God's mighty hands worked another miracle in my life. I was in bed, thanking the Lord for sending my sister back home just in time. God gave me another chance at life, and I gave God praise for my husband, my darling sister and my sweet little alarms, Curtis and Cary, Jr.

MICHAEL
CHAPTER SEVEN

Upon leaving South Carolina to go north with Uncle and family, Sister left looking very matronly and plain, but when she returned one year later, she had the figure of a coke bottle, and as the Commodores referenced in their song, she was a brick house. She went from old-looking to vah-va-va-voom, which meant young men would be knocking at our door to see the star beauty.

Our home would have male visitors all the time particularly with Cary being a mechanic, and one of seven brothers. However, when other young men started to come around to see Lucille, I feared she could end up getting hurt by shenanigans. However, I had to admit, I wanted her to lead a normal life and experience the love of a man, marriage, and a family, knowing she was capable of such. She was an excellent homemaker, a dynamic cook, and she loved children.

About 16 miles from where we lived, a young man named James Moments, from Blackville, SC, noticed Lucille at afternoon gospel programs. She was captivating to so many men in the area but as the old saying goes, you snooze, you lose and the early bird gets the worm. After seeing her many times, James began his pursuit of her, making small talks at the program. From there he came to our home to keep company with her. She was happy and excited. They would share the movies, walks, talks, and other small gestures.

They became exclusively a couple after a few short visits. From all appearances, it was love at first sight. I wanted to be happy for her but I had great apprehensions. I was so afraid because I felt he was overlooking her apparent challenges. I was afraid her beauty could have clouded Mr. Moment's judgment. If you didn't know her, you wouldn't be able to tell she had deficiencies.

James and Lucille seemed in love. In fact, Cary and my relationship started much the same way. I hoped for the best and I knew I needed to have a talk with him.

He hadn't been dating Lucille longer than a New York minute and already, he's talking about marriage to my sister. I wasn't sure of how to approach him, but I knew it had to be done. Sometimes in love, you have to make some tough love decisions, and it was one of the hardest things I had to do. I hoped he would understand my intentions were not to stop their relationship, but he came back with a force on his convictions and care for my sister. He informed me that he didn't care about any problems or condition Lucille had. He would love her no matter what. He made sure to let me know I wasn't Lucille's mother. He said he was going to marry her, she was GOING TO BE HIS WIFE, and he was going to be responsible for her, "and that was it."
After that speech, all I could do was seal it with a prayer

and hope for the best. They dated for two short months, then they got hitched at the county courthouse mid-June 1963. They moved in with us and stayed until Cary, the children and I moved out in about a month or so to our new house.

Four to five months later, the newlyweds moved near James' mother in Blackville, South Carolina. I felt so much better knowing they were living closer to his mother. His mother treated Lucille with kindness and respect, which brought me comfort.

Time passed and I kept in touch with my sister and our brother. We found out that Lucille was pregnant. She had the hereditary pre-eclampsia as our mother and me. Even though she had difficulty in the pregnancy, she delivered a 7 lb. 5 oz. baby boy named Michael. James was there to support and uphold his wife and child. Lucille was the happiest woman on the planet the day she gave birth to her own child. She always wanted children, and now she and James had a little boy. This precious little baby brought Lucille to life. I kept in touch and helped her out with the baby when I could.

Now that Lucille and James were building their family tree, my fears didn't raise its ugly head quite as much. Baby Michael, I prayed, would be the catalyst for their marriage. Their love for this child would be a holding point for them in marriage.

Little Michael had grown to be a year old and was walking, when James announced that he wanted to move closer to us. Their search brought his family to a little home near Bamberg, very near to us. I was glad about because Lucille and I always felt the need to be close to each other. It was when we were apart that made me feel as if something was missing.

Motherhood, for us, was a blessing because we helped each other. Just as we were getting comfortable, James made announced his plans to move to D.C. for another job with his brothers. I was thinking, if life isn't broken, why fix it? Things were going so well, we thought; new family new house, and a good job working in the logging business.

His mother didn't want them to go and neither did Lucille or I. Premonition is a mysterious thing. God gives mothers an intuition for their children, but God gave me intuition for my sister. James was a smooth and fast talker even from the beginning. We tried to change his mind, but his mind was made up. When they left for the city, I was worried about Lucille being so far away. All I could do was ask my Lord to instruct, teach and guide her with his eyes. Her husband told me not to worry because he would take care of her, so I turned them over to the Lord.

Meanwhile, Cary and Legrand Hallman were friends that worked and sang together. His wife Emma and I became great friends. Our men searched for better employment while still working on Bossman's farms in two different locations.

It was mid-July when our husbands finally found new jobs at J. F. Clerkly and Company doing road construction work. This meant they would be away from home all but one day a week, and for us, it was well worth to get off that farm. Emma and I started house hunting, while our husbands were away working in Augusta, GA. This was the first time since marriage we were separated from our spouses with eight head of children. We each had four children, I had 3 boys and one girl and she had the very opposite. We laughed about that many days. We had the best of many awful times. She and I were very close, raising our children together. We shared whatever we had with one another.

Wednesday, our men started their new job without old Bossman's knowledge. Bright and early the next morning, Emma and I went house hunting at our husbands advise. We found the two houses we were told about. One big house with electricity and a small house was without. I accepted the lesser. At that time, anything was better than being where we were.

Bossman came looking for his underpaid, overworked, prized possessions; our husbands. He asked angrily, "Where is Cary and them?" We withheld the truth, "They ain't here." "Well, way dey at?" "I don't know!" We might have been born at night but not last night. We weren't going to divulge any information for him to react to.

The next day while the men were working in Augusta, old Bossman came back again looking for his workers, with the same questions, and I gave him the same answers. He told me, "if Cary ain't back to work on Monday morning, I want my house back!" I know he thought he was doing something, but God had it fixed up. When our husbands got home Saturday morning, the truck was at the door of that house and we were all moving out to our little piece of the pie. Now, it was no easy road in our little mansions, but we made it work and was willing to endure. At night fall, we lived with Emma and her children, who had electricity.

Cary and I continued looking for a home with electricity, and found a home near the Bamberg River. Cary's parents were highly opposed to us living near the river because they were afraid of the children drowning. They continued to look for houses until they were satisfied their grandchildren were safe. They found a small four room house on Edisto Drive not far from them. When Cary came home from work that weekend, we packed up and moved to that four room shot-gun house near his parents.

Granny taught me a wonderful trade that I always loved, she taught me how to sew. I was good at it and it was a great passion of mine, not to mention I wanted to help Cary out as much as possible.

There were quite a few manufacturing companies in the surrounding areas like Denmark, Bamberg, and

Orangeburg. I applied for work, but it wasn't until 1966 that sewing positions opened for coloreds.

I could sew with the best of them, but the only positions available for women of color were cleaning or service work. However, I kept my hopes high with the faith I would be hired as a sewing operator in one of the sewing rooms. All I needed was a chance to prove myself, but I heard the same statement every time I applied, "we're looking for experienced operators." I had my sewing papers of experience right from the Rosetta Ross Grant School of Sewing, my Granny!

When I heard the industry was offering classes, I jumped at the chance. I took the opportunity and filled out an application for the training classes at Orangeburg Sewing Manufacturing Company and on the second Thursday in December, 1966, I became in high demand. Door Manufacturing Company in Denmark, SC called that morning and Orangeburg Sewing Manufacturing that afternoon. Each company wanted me to report to work on the following Monday, but I chose the Orangeburg Sewing Company because I wanted their experience. They had a two-week training class of which I only trained one week before being hired. I worked about five months. Then Ambler Industries, another sewing company with greater benefits and lower productions, called. I signed on with them and starting making men's coat backs called vents, but soon I was doing almost any job detail requested. I was skilled on anything they gave me. I continued with the company until the mid-1980's. We were blessed and grateful for the two incomes. Three of our four children were in school and his mother and nephew cared for our other children while we worked.

I kept in touch with Johnny and Lucille as often as I could. It had been about a year or more since Lucille and James moved to D.C. When I spoke to her, she assured me everything was okay. I wanted to believe she was happy, but that feeling of unrest would not go away. I just had a strange feeling that things weren't good. I would wake up in the midnight hours and pray for her and her family. Tears would come to my eyes when I was not really crying. Night after night I could not shake the feeling of unrest.

A hot summer's day in 1967, Lucille and a close friend were together with their children in her apartment. She would visit her on a regular basis. They would watch out for each other's sons. Michael and his young friend were about the same age. Michael and his buddy were playing when the ice cream truck drove up. Lucille and her friend would take turns going for ice cream. The friends lived in an apartment and it was Lucille's turn to get ice cream for the boys. She asked her friend to watch out for her son while she went downstairs for the ice cream as she always did, and the friend agreed. But the unspeakable happened. Michael came down the stairs behind his mother, unbeknownst to her. His Dad was standing in the back yard but didn't notice him either. As she crossed the street and stood by the ice cream truck, she heard the squealing of tires. When she looked back, she saw the blue coat Michael was wearing. A car was dragging her little boy.

That night the phone rang. I answered to bad news. My only nephew, my sister's only child struck and dragged by a car. Michael, before his third birthday, was pronounced dead. All I could say was, "Oh Lord, help her." I thought about the condition of my sister and wondered how could she see that and take it. I just knew it was a horrible scene. His parents brought his body back south for his burial. When I looked upon my sister's face, I saw all the pain and grief she was in. Michael meant everything to Lucille. He was her heart string.

This was one of the most difficult times that I ever had with her. All I could do was hold her in my arms and let her know I was there for her. He was all she could have. She loved children so much and the tragedy was, she could not have any other children.

We, as family, were there for Lucille and her husband. After Michael's funeral, Lucille & James returned to Washington, D.C. She lived there for about six months before she realized she couldn't take living there anymore. Lucille didn't want to move back south without James. Her health started to fail. Most of that was because she blamed herself for Michael's death. James insisted she move back south, so she returned broken, shabby and lost. It was a dark time in all of our lives.

Granny's words would always come back to me just at the right time. She'd say, "Behind every dark cloud, the sun will surely shine again." I just kept watching, praying, and waiting, and our strength was renewed day by day.

We attended church on a regular basis for spiritual guidance. We still visited Johnny as much as possible. I enjoyed going to work because it would take my mind off my problems and gave me something good to think about. I kept reminding Lucille of Granny's words, "We are not alone, no matter what we have to face in life." I continued to encourage her, "the Lord is with us," as the Scriptures promised.

After the death of Michael, my sister's health worsened. Her condition was mainly with her stomach and weight. She had seen many doctors, and was hospitalized. She had numerous fibroid tumors removed, but many others were not, because they would endanger her life. Even though gripping and nagging pain were her constant companion for two years or more, she had a high tolerance for pain. Lucille was incredibly strong when it came to dealing with pain.

I prayed for her daily that she would rise from this sickness. The LORD did answer my prayer. On Friday, May, 10, 2002, Lucille and I took a stroll, laughing, talking, and enjoyed the fresh evening breeze. We shared a delectable meal together. Everything about this Friday was perfect. Little did I know it would be our last, because the next morning, she woke up in the presence of the Lord without suffering and lamentation. I was left alone, but this Scripture was my comfort –

"Fear thou not; for I am with thee: be not dismayed; for I am thy God: I will strengthen thee; yea, I will help thee; yea, I will uphold thee with the right hand of my righteousness."
Isaiah 41:10

JOYFUL TIMES

The weekends were the only time Cary, the children and I would spend time together. We used our time wisely when Cary's quartet group was not traveling. We used every chance we could to take family outings to Santee Park, Sweet Water Lake, Six Flags Over Georgia, and Carowinds to name a few. Seeing my husband enjoying his children made me realize how grateful I was. I had a lot to live for. I didn't have these opportunities with my parents.

My desire was for our family to be close-knit. Cary and I loved to visit family on a regular basis and our children loved to get together with their cousins to play. I got joy out of seeing them enjoy one another. Cary and his brothers saw their parents practically every Sunday, even if they had a musical gig. One of Cary's brother's children was close to our kids ages. When the wives didn't travel with the husbands for singing, we would get together.

I wanted to make sure my children knew their family because as a child, my siblings and I grew up without knowing our family. I taught my children to know, be close to, and respect their family, particularly their elders. When we couldn't visit, we'd call one another to keep the lines of communication open.

CONSPIRACY

I thank God for Granny's words that came back to me in a trying time, *"believe half of what your eyes see and nothing of what you hear-say until it is proven. Man will put you down, but the Lord will pick you up and He will stand by you when the going gets tough."* This was one of the most startling events of my marriage. I started receiving anonymous phone calls. The caller would tell me she was a friend of mine, she wanted to alert me of my husband having an affair, as she put it, "your husband is not treating you right. He is not going to sing, but Cary and his woman are going to the White Cloud Club." She continued, "If you don't believe me, I can tell you exactly what he was wearing." She described him from head to toe. "Go now, if you want to catch him. You will find them at the club." I thanked her and told her I was going to check it out, but I never once left my house.

The caller created a segment of doubt for me. Yes, I know my husband, I know what he looks like when he went singing. I would be with him and see the sweat from his brow to his back, so coming home drenched was never a surprise, it was part of the process. When I questioned him at first, his gentleness would calm me right down, by saying, "Yes, people saw me, but not at no club."

This conspiracy went on for about three months or more. Every Sunday I didn't go to the program; I would receive that mystery call. The caller would say, I could find them at one of the two clubs, The White Cloud or the Delmorockco Club. I didn't know where either club was, even if I was silly enough to search it out, but I wasn't remotely interested in finding out. As the song says, *"You can't make me doubt Him, because I KNOW too much about Him!"* I knew my husband, but I have to admit, I was very confused by the calls. The caller who tried to break up my marriage wouldn't say to Cary, whom she said she saw up close, "Cary, why are you doing this to your wife? You better go home, or else I'm gonna tell her what you're doing." Instead she would call me to say I was too nice a person to be mistreated. She described my husband's outfits almost down to his socks. Hmm, I wondered, is she the one?

One Sunday evening when Cary came home from singing, I lit into him heavily about the mysterious caller and what she said she saw. My husband tried to assure and reassure me that what I was being told was not true. I didn't know what to think. I can truly say the going had gotten tough, but I continued to ask the Lord for knowledge concerning this anonymous caller.

I never mentioned my concerned to any other person except my husband, and the Lord. I believed the answer would to be revealed to me, so I just waited and waited. After many anonymous calls, the answer came one Sunday evening. *Ms. Mysterious* usually called about 30 minutes to an hour after the men left for their program, but this Sunday, she called about ten minutes after the men left. The caller told me to go to Delmorockco Club and I would find him and his lady there, but as the caller was talking to me, I heard the sound of a little toy train in the background. The sound was so familiar to me, but I couldn't remember where I'd heard that sound. When she finished gossiping, I thanked her as I always did. Then it came to me, the epiphany. Our children played with a little toy train that sounded just like the sound from the phone caller. That sound from the caller's house was from one of the girls in the inner circle. I was speechless, flabbergasted, and knocked for a loop. I turned the tides by asking, "Did anyone from your house call me about ten minutes ago?" She assured me that no one did. I asked her were her children playing with their little toy train and she said "yes, they're back there playing." Then I told her that an anonymous caller, whom said she was my friend, had been calling me a while and that same caller called me again about ten minutes ago. I told her everything the caller said and as the caller was talking I heard that same little toy train sound. She said no one made a call from her house, but after that Sunday, I never received another call from Ms. Mysterious.

I was hurt and deeply offended, but I never said anything else concerning the mystery caller and the woman from the inner circle did the same without even an apology. Every time I heard the sound of that toy chu-chu train, I thought of that conspiracy, but God helped me continue with everyone in the inner circle as if nothing had happened simply because I knew it would have cost the relationship of our little children and they would have suffered the most. The meaning of the word conspiracy, i.e. a vicious plot to harm another. Now I see why God's word says,

"A man's foes shall be they of his own household."
Matthew 10:36

"Trust you not in a friend, put not confidence in a guide: (men) keep the door of thy mouth from them that lies in thy bosom."
Micah 7:5,6

When I first read these Scriptures, my understanding was dull, but not anymore. They have since blessed me. Through a spiritual eye of discernment, His word is not telling us to dishonor our people, but what He is saying is:

"Trust in the LORD with all thine heart; and lean not unto your own understanding, but in all thy ways acknowledge Him and He shall direct thy path." **Proverbs 3:5,6**

I was so grateful to the Lord for how he delivered me. I didn't understand how I was able to keep my cool at that time. Now I know, as the Apostle Paul says in **Philippians 2:13**, *"For it is God which works in you both to will and to do of His good pleasure."* He was working in and through me, instructing, teaching, and guiding me all the way.

"The joy of the LORD, (His Word) is your strength,
Nehemiah 8:10b

Ethel G. Wade

KNOWLEDGE OF THE GENERATIONAL CURSE
CHAPTER EIGHT

Over the years of having a relationship with my father's siblings, it became more apparent to me the condition that caused my mother's death. I had been told that our mother's nerves had gotten so bad before she expired, that they believed it caused her death. I knew deep down in my heart that I needed to know more about my mother's condition and her side of the family because my brother and sister had been affected by the same problem. Also, I am seeing the same patterns in my daughter and her son's behavior. I needed to find out more in order to know what to look out for or to avoid.

When we found our father's people, they told us some things concerning him, but our mother's people never seemed to want to talk about our mother. I tried finding a photograph of her. Everyone told me to just look in the mirror because I looked just like her. I had to accept that, but I was only three when Mother died, and now that I'm a grown woman, looking in the mirror didn't pacify me. I longed for answers about my mother. Family members told me to leave the mother subject alone, which was shocking to me. I wondered why they tried to close my mother's life with a comment that she had a nervous condition as she carried us.

After attending a Bible teaching church, I learned so much, and was greatly intrigued by the subject of generational curses! I saw in the Scripture **Hosea 4:6**, "*My people are destroyed for a lack of knowledge*: not knowing what has happened in the past because thou hast rejected knowledge, He says, "*I will also reject thee, and thy children.*" I thank God for embracing knowledge. I asked for knowledge as King Solomon asked, and I was interested in the knowledge of my legacy and heritage. Many people had told me to leave my mother's history alone, but that made me more curious. It was as if I was one of the blind men in **Matthew 20:30**, "*two blind men asked the Lord to have mercy on them, because they wanted to see. And the multitude of people told them to shut up.*"

Henry Jamison holding Baby Bunion Jamison and Essie (grandparents)

The pastor of Cedar Grove Baptist Church had connections with some churches in the north, so we began traveling every other year to Washington, DC, and Philadelphia, PA on a regular basis. We had many joyful times. I used these outing to research my family history and I had great hopes of meeting someone who knew something about my mother's lineage. Every place I'd go, I'd asked questions, but would get bits and pieces of information; yet nothing significant enough to say I had any solid leads. It would just be the typical, "let sleeping dogs lie" conversations, or "look in the mirror, you are the splitting image of your Momma."

Then something happened! I remember distinctly while living near the dairy on old Bossman's place, having a disturbing premonition. I awoke up early one Thursday morning and for some reason, my good old Aunt Essie was on my mind. I just felt so depressed like I wanted to cry. I could not go back to sleep that morning. I just laid there wondering if she was ill. I remember what Granny told me many times that the Lord was going to show me my troubles before they come. I just tossed and turned until daylight. When my husband woke up, I told him how I felt. I wanted to call her that day, but I couldn't because I didn't have her number and we didn't have a home phone. Thursday and Friday that feeling of doom and depression was on me like a soiled raincoat.

In my restlessness, I got Aunt Essie's number from a cousin and went about a mile from the house to use the old pay phone at the corner store to call Aunt Essie. Rev. Bunion Jamison, known around town as BJ, answered the phone; he's Aunt Essie's son. He told me his mother was very sick. Cary said, "Let's go and see her." Cary wanted me to find my people as well as I. We headed to Asheville, North Carolina on Saturday, praying God would keep her. When we arrived at her house, Cousin BJ Jamison told us his mother was in the nursing home, far from their home. He wanted us to just remember our aunt as she was. He didn't want us to see her in her present condition. I didn't care how far the nursing home was, or how sick she was, I wanted to see her.

When we arrived, I begged him to let me see her. His wife was on our side too, saying, "honey, why don't you take them to see her?" Although his stubbornness won, and he would not let us see my aunt, we continued to beg until we left Monday morning. He refused our every request to see his mother. I couldn't believe he would deny me the joy of seeing my favorite aunt. I was hurt and confused. Why didn't he want us to see her?"

I cried almost all the way home between nodding and thinking a lot, but saying very few words. I had a feeling that Aunt Essie had something to say or something to give, but he was trying to prevent it from happening. I felt hollow, as if I had lost someone very dear to me. I continued praying and asking God to help me understand why my feelings towards this aunt were so strong. **Isaiah 40:31a**, says, *"but they that wait upon the LORD shall renew their strength."* As I waited, I got my answer.

Working in the field with lots of my family members, and talking to others, led me to information about the kinship of Charlie Jamison's family. We kept in touch with them, and we found out that Cousin Charlie's wife wasn't well, so Lucille and I went to visit Cousin Jessie Mae on her sick bed. We visited with her briefly because we could see she was very weak. My sister and I also spoke with Cousin Charlie, who was in his mid–seventies. He was very open so we talked about many things, including my mother's side of the family.

As we continued to talk, I told him about Aunt Essie, who had been so good to us as children, and how the Lord had put her on my mind. We spoke about the trip Cary and I took to Asheville, North Carolina. I continued with the emptiness I felt in my heart. Then he said, "Mae?" I replied, "Sir?" He said, "No one ever told you?" I replied, "Told me what?" He said, "I will tell you what happened and let you figure it out. Aunt Essie had two young babies; a little boy (Bunion Jamison) and a little girl (Rosetta Jamison). She brought them down south for her sister Alnora, who was married to your father, to keep. Henry, my father's brother, and the lady you call Aunt Essie were actually your grandparents."

"Oh me! Oh my! O Lord No! You don't have to say anything else. We were always told that our Grandmother was Alnora and our Aunt Essie brought two young children to the south for her sister Alnora to keep." He said, "no," and he repeated the story once again to be sure I was very clear. Your Aunt Essie brought her two little children to her sister Alnora, who was married to your dad. They raised your mother. Your Aunt Alnora later died."

After all this time, I finally found out the truth! It turns out that my cousin was my uncle. The whole time my Aunt Essie was my Grandmother and I didn't know it. These were secrets in my family that I didn't know until I was grown.

The Root of it all

In Genesis, the Bible mentions multiplication and procreation. With there being only two original people on the earth, populating was not possible without incest. In fact, there were even six famous writings about it from the Holy Writ beginning with Adam and Eve's children and throughout our existence where history evolves over and over again. Greek Mythology speaks of incestuous relationships, but for this to happen in my own family was a bit much for me to digest. Here is my family bloodline:

Edmond Grant and Big Rosetta Grant (Great Granny married and had nine children; two boys, seven girls: (1) Wally, (2) Eulisha (3) Edmond, (4) Lillie, (5) Cora, (6) Alnora, (7) Essie (Isabella), (8) Hattie Sue, (9) Ollie. Essie and Henry Jamison had three children, Bunion (BT), my mother; Little Rosetta and one other child who didn't survive.

Knowing the family history helps me better understand why my mother, Little Rosetta, had a nervous condition. I see now it was because she was forced to marry the man she called father, Freddie Gordon, and Little Rosetta gave birth to Johnny, Lucille, and me. I was essentially named after the woman who stole my heart as a little girl. I was told she was an aunt, but now I know, she was my grandmother. Her name was Essie and my name was Effia.

As Cousin Charlie went on to tell the whole story, I was in shock! He said, "Your mother ran away from home many times because her step-daddy, who in actuality was her uncle in-law, turned his affections towards her." It was completely apparent to me, why my mother had this nervous problem. The man we knew as our father actually raised my mother. She loved him as a father, and not as a lover, but he wanted more. Family members tried to persuade her to follow through or she would lose her inheritance. They wanted her to focus on marriage for the sake of land, a house, and some other measly things. Whether his motives were pure or not, our father made a terrible mistake, because he lacked Biblical knowledge found in **Leviticus 18**. Little Rosetta wouldn't dream of doing that so she continued running. Her timing ran out from trying to escape marriage. He had won. Unfortunately, the land nor the big house did them any good. They lost it all as their lives were cut short." He fell from a building after our mother's death.

Concealing knowledge is just as devastating as the lack of knowledge. Some things we should be discreet about, but there are other things we should reveal to our children because holding vital information will devastate and destroy more than protect. *"My people are destroyed for lack of knowledge."* **Hosea 4:6**

God blessed me to see clearly with the eye of discernment after wondering for so long. I see why the Lord took my mother to her resting place so early in our lives, she was only 26 years when she died. My answer was in ***Isaiah 57:1-2***, *"The righteous perish and no man lay it to heart, and merciful men are taken away, none considering the righteous in taken away from the evil to come."* When I read that verse I felt a burden lift. I just thanked the LORD for giving me the answers to many of my childhood questions. I believe He spared my mother from seeing her children suffer because of the forced decision made by her stepdad. God allowed her to enter into peace, resting in her Heavenly bed.

Bunion, the son of my real Grandmother (Aunt Essie), concealed her death and came to see us afterwards. The nerve of him not to even tell us she died; not a word about her passing.

I confronted him about the matter regarding my mother and grandmother. During the conversation, he didn't say a word, NOTHING!
He did ask who told me, and I let him know. He was at a loss for words and avoided confirming the truth about what I learned. He returned home, and we never saw him alive again. He died in a car crash in N.C.

*"He'll bring the father's iniquity (their spiritual weakness) upon the children, children's children to the third and fourth generation. **Exodus 20:5; 34:7***

Jeremiah 32:18;

(God says what He means, and means what He says)

*"So shall my word be that goes forth out of my mouth: it shall not return unto me void, but it shall accomplish (do what I says) that which I please, and it shall prosper in the thing whereto I send it. **Isaiah 55:11**.*

Now I understood why I, my siblings, and my children have these nerve conditions. This is from a generation of sins passed down that needed to be confessed and broken.

These afflictions, curses and sins can only be broken by the word of God and prayer which will set us apart from them, through sanctification. *1 Timothy 4:5*. God is faithful to forgive these spiritual weaknesses that are bound inside of the hearts of men. He sent his SON to remove them **Acts 3:26**. God will bring our wrong-doings upon our children, children's children as He did on King Saul's seven grandsons. **1 Kings 21: 1, 9.**

MY YOUNG ADULTS
CHAPTER NINE

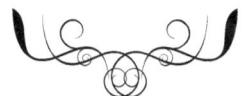

I KNOW PRAYER WORKS

As a Minister, I was beginning to understand better every day, what goes on in many families. Family relationships are very important. God created man and woman and when children come out of that love union, there is a strong responsibility on the parents, to nurture them naturally, emotionally, and spiritually. The first ministry is family. If the family is not secure, then our neighborhoods and communities will not be stable. If our communities are not stable, our cities and states will subsequently be out of whack. An out of whack city or state will bleed into chaos and uncontrollable immorality. Work is important in the home, but communication is far more important than money and things. If a family does not have a sense of community in the confines of its home, they essentially have nothing.

Cary worked away from home practically every week, while I kept everything together on the home front. The children weren't getting any younger, and neither were we. They were growing like weeds into teens and needed their father more than ever; especially the boys. Working and praying for my husband to get a job with better hours was my duty. Cary's job kept him away from home all week long, sometimes six days a week, but I needed him home at night to talk to his sons. Cary began his search for another job.

My prayers were answered when he found a job at Smith Corona Manufacturing Company (SCMC) in Orangeburg, SC. At this company, Cary worked regular eight hour days which allowed him to be home at nights. It was a refreshing and good change after eight years of doing construction work. He continued working at SCMC until they closed, October 1973. He was later hired at Greenwood Mills. The downfall of this employment was second shift. Anybody who has worked this shift knows how debilitating it is. You're working when everything good is happening. We didn't particularly like the midnight work, because it made communication between him and the boys virtually impossible. However, we were thankful for the job. Young men need the teaching and experiences from their father. Cary would look in on them when he came in at night. To help keep the lines of communication open, he would wake the boys and talk with them about what was going on with them. I reflected on another one of granny's most inspiring words, "Communication is to a family like blood is to the body."

Without communication, a family is spiritually dead. They can and will fall for anything. **Proverbs 11:14**

...and their purposes for a prosperous life can, and will be lost."
Proverbs 15:22

These little people God gave us were now growing up to be teenagers. It was now the summer of 1974 and Zener Mae was 17, Cary Jr. was 15, Curtis was 14 and Rodney was 11 years old. I was looking at my daughter going out on dates and my sons getting ready to follow in her footsteps. I reminded myself of the good times we had on family outings, going places together like Santee Park, Sweetwater Lake, and Myrtle Beach. We even had some joyful church outings to Myrtle Beach. Times like those are what kept me going through my troubles. While watching them go out into the world on their own was indeed a blessing, it was also a frightening time. I told them like Granny used to tell us, if you are out with friends never drink out of a glass or cup you left on a table unattended.

I knew their father's time was limited with them, but when he would speak, like E.F. Hutton, they listened. We taught our children to love and respect all people, regardless of whether they were young or old and despite any disabilities. We taught them not to look down on anyone unless they were picking them up. We taught them to love, not because they were loved, but because "God commands us to love." **John 15:17**.

Granny taught us not to ever insult or disrespect our elders, but treat them as fathers and mothers. She was quoting Scriptures, **Exodus 20:12** *"Honor thy father and thy mother: that thy days may be long upon the land which the lord thy God gives thee."* She also quoted **Matthew 15:4**, which says, *"For God commanded, saying honor thy father and thy*

Mother; and he who curses father or mother, let him die the death." – (meaning, that Satan curse of death is open to them, when their parent's necessities called for their assistance, and they pleaded that all they could spare was devoted to the treasure of the temple, and therefore their parents must expect nothing from them (quoted) from the Matthew Henry Bible). This is what my Granny was saying, when she told us never tear down the old bridge that brought you across safe, you may need that old bridge to come back across; meaning ***never forget what the elders have done for you, when you couldn't do!***

In addition to working on my job, I also had to maintain the house. I'd prepare the meals, get their clothes ready the next day, and make sure their homework was done.

My personal sewing room gave me such joy and my high work ethic caused me to lose track of time. I would sew until the early hours of the morning.

My children and my work were my pride and joy. Sewing was like child's play to me. I wanted my children to look their best at all times. My mind was at ease while occupied. I would rather sew than eat, making many leisure suits and outfits for my husband and my sons.

Our oldest son won Best Dressed once at school. I even made his prom suit. My daughter's clothes took just a snap of my fingers to make. I made a lot of their clothing from 1972 through 1980 until my youngest son graduated from high school. Granny taught me to sew, and I just loved it!

Although we had some good times and some bad times, family relationships made it all doable and livable. We taught the children to talk things out and not to let problems get out of hand. Cary Jr. was now driving school buses to make extra spending money.

Although, my husband and I never bought our children name brand clothes, they went out looking good. When they started making their own little money they bought what they wanted.

Seeing them grow into young adults was a blessing to me. I kept them in prayer when they went out. My faith wasn't strong enough to allow me sweet sleep, until they returned home. Cary tried convincing me the children would be alright and for me to get my rest, but it was always easier said than done.

I kept hoping for the best and encouraging them when they went out, to use their own minds, especially my daughter, who was easy-going like her father. She also reminded me of my sister, never having much to say. I also continued to stand in the gap for Cary while he was on the road singing.

I prayed for everyone, but I could tell my body was tired. I knew that I had to find a way to let go and let God take control. I taught them well, and I needed to be able to rest when they were away from me.

Curtis assisted me greatly around the house. One day we were nailing a board back in place on our fence in the front yard. I thought I had control of the hammer, but when the hammer separated from the wood, it flew off and caught him under his left eye, leaving a deep gash. When I saw the blood, I thought the hammer hit my son in the eye and knocked it out. I was scared almost out of my skin. I took him to the hospital for stitches and he was okay.

It is the fall of 1974, and both school and football season were back in session. All three of our sons loved sports, but our oldest son Cary Jr. was an all-around sportsman. He played both basketball and football.

The boys had their driver's licenses, and wanted to show that alpha male control by not riding together to the ball games. The boy's dad was at work and I felt a little restless until they got home. I stood by the window in my bedroom. I remember the prayer that I prayed, "Lord, you gave us these four children. You helped us to bring them up to this point, and now they are young adults going out into this world. Lord, I cannot be out there with them, but You are! Now Lord, you gave them to us and now I'm giving them back to You. Please help me to let go and let You take control, so I can get some rest." As I stood there meditating, it happened. I heard in my spirit, "go and make extra keys and pray over them. Give them a key and remind them of their curfew. As you Pray, don't worry. Go in your bed and get your rest." I thought, oh my, give them a key? I realized I wouldn't have to get up and let them in at night. I talked to Cary about what I heard and he said, "If it will help you to get some rest and not worry, do it."

We talked with them about having keys, meeting curfew and being responsible. Zener, Rodney, Curtis, and Cary promised we would not have to worry. They were encouraged to ride together as much as possible.

Thank goodness! I was finally at peace and my rest was sweet. I gave my children back to God and got my freedom. I gave them independence and the apron string was cut. Relieved by trusting God, our children showed us honor by keeping their word. When Cary and I would check on them, they were all in bed. The keys didn't change our family statutes at all.

They could use the family car for their outings, but the stipulation was to attend Sunday school and church. When Cary and I were not at our church for service, the children willingly attended. We respected them, and they respected us.

Son Foot Ball Injury:

It was the beginning of the football practice season in 1977. Cary Jr. played defensive end for his school team, the Edisto Cougars. He was so excited to be a senior high football player. It was one of the first games and he wanted me to come and watch him do his thing with the team, but not feeling well, I was unable to attend. I wasn't a big football fan, but I supported my children's activities as much as possible. It frightened me to see them play because they seem to hit each other with vengeance. Cary rode out to the game to see his son's play. An hour or so into the game, my phone rang with Cary on the other end saying, "Mae, meet me at the hospital. Junior got blind-sided on the field, but He's gonna be alright." My blood rushed straight to my head, and I began to panic. Cary knew how to calm me down, so I could at least drive the car to the hospital. What he didn't tell me was Cary Jr, was knocked slam out on the field.

My imagination went in every way possible; blood, stitches, casts and screams of pain, "Mom-mah, help me." I was grateful Cary didn't tell me everything over the phone. The impact from the hit tore the ligaments in his right knee. I didn't know what to expect, but when I got to the hospital, there Junior was, sitting in the room just as cool and calm as a cucumber without pain. When he saw me he said, "Mom, look," while he pushed his knee from one side to the other, under the skin. The movement was gross and free. Given the condition his knee was in; it was indeed a miracle that he had no pain. The doctor told us he had seen many young men with the same type of knee injury, but never had he seen anyone who wasn't in great pain. They performed emergency surgery that same night and when it was over, he was still without pains. It was a blessing from Heaven. I do believe it had a lot to do with me being baptized in my fifth month of carrying him. Five is the number of revival and grace. To God be the glory!

After spending a little time in the hospital, he was released to go home with strict orders to stay off the injured leg for 30-60 days. Junior didn't want to hear that,

It was the end of his high school football season and he was now on crutches. He had hopes of being off crutches by the basketball season. Time flew by and we were elated to see Cary Jr. progress as fast as he did. He never complained of pain.

Basketball season had come and Junior was off crutches and doing fine. The doctor discharged him but warned him that he may have problems with the knee if he played basketball too early because the muscle may not be strong enough to take the pressure. He warned us that the knee could slip out of joint and not go back in. That would mean emergency surgery all over again.

The doctor gave him a band to put around his knee when he played. Against the physician's strong advice not to start back too quickly, Cary began Basketball practice. Everything went well for a while, after playing two or three games his knee started to slip out of place. This happened many times as he was playing. We wanted him to stop, but he wanted to prove that winners never quit and quitters never win. He wouldn't give up until that knee slipped out of joint and wouldn't go back in place. He was feeling some pain, and couldn't walk. He was brought home on crutches.

I called the doctor and he said for Cary to lie down and keep his leg elevated with pillows and bring him to the office early Monday morning. He told us to be prepared for Cary Jr. to undergo surgery, and of course we didn't want to hear that.

The doctor told me that it was going to swell a lot but not to be alarmed. The next morning, Cary's knee had swollen up larger than his head! It hurt to look at, and touching it was impossible. This was the first time he showed any sign of pain. I prayed for him, and hoped for a miracle. No one wanted him to go through another surgical procedure.

Sunday Morning, when dad, the other boys and I got to church, I wrote a note to the pastor asking him to please call my son's name in prayer. I felt that if my pastor called his name in prayer at church, then maybe he wouldn't have to go through surgery. I waited to hear my son's name, but he never called Cary's name.

A lot was going on that morning, as it was the first pastoral appreciation. His prayers were beautiful, but to my disappointment, did not include my son.

After the service, I was sure I was wearing frustration on my brow as I greeted a few people including the pastor and his wife on the way to our car. I don't know that seeing me even reminded him that I'd asked for prayer and that made me even more angry, but we're not supposed to be angry at the pastor, right? On the way home, I told Cary the whole story and he assured me everything was going to be alright with Jr.

When we got to our street, I heard the Holy Ghost say, "Go pray for your own son." When Cary pulled up in our driveway, I told everyone to meet in Junior's room for prayer.

We knelt down, I placed my hand on that swollen knee, and I called on the name of the Lord in prayer for my son. I looked at that swollen knee and we left the room. Rodney and Curtis stayed. Before I could reach the stove in my kitchen, my son called out to me, out of great pain, "Awe Momma, my knee! my knee." I was lost for words. I paused at that moment in apprehension! He yelled out, "My knee popped back in place, Momma!" My young man got up and met me down the hall on his crutches on that swollen knee. What a day! Our family saw a miracle that day! After seeing my son's knee back in place, all I could say was God did it and thank you Lord!

He said, "Mom, Curtis and Rodney started playing with me. They were throwing the pillows from their bed. When they ran out of pillows they grabbed the pillow from under my leg and my knee popped back in place."

After hearing this, I didn't know whether to choke them or kiss them. I was so grateful; I couldn't get angry at the boys because their brother's knee was back in place. We still didn't know what the doctor was going to say concerning the surgery that Monday morning, but one thing we did know was that Junior's knee was back in place and he was up and walking.

By Monday most of the swelling was gone. I took him to the doctor with high hopes he wouldn't need surgery. The doctor's examination proved what we prayed in faith. The doctor looked at Cary saying, "young man, you don't need surgery. Your x-rays look fine." The acts of God's powerful hands worked through family prayer, and his two young brothers.

A short time after that, Cary Jr. wanted a motorcycle but I felt strongly against him having one. Unfortunately, I lost that battle. One beautiful day in the summer of 1977, Junior and his friends decided to go for a joy ride. Dressed in their bike-riding garb of black and denim, helmets and gloves, and a whole lot of vroom, vroom, they were off. The biking friends put the rubber to the road, as they were joyriding on their motorcycle on Highway 301. They came to a stop at Stonewall Jackson crossing. Cary told me his bike was number seven. Six of the motorcycles passed through the intersection, then a car pulled right out in front of his bike. He told me a thought came to him to jump! He jumped and slid across the hood of that car. Our son returned home with minor bruises on his arms and stomach, but his bike was a total loss. Another miracle! I know prayer works!

Cary was of dating age. He courted one of the young flowers at his school. One cool evening he went to visit his girl, but met a family of deer on the way. The car crashed into the family of three. I shared with my children, things Granny told us to do in troubled times. She said if an animal runs out in front of your moving car, do what you can do to miss the animal or whatever. If you can't avoid the animal, take your foot off the accelerator, hold your steering wheel as tight as you can and do not jam on your brakes.

My son remembered what I told him. He said mom, "I took my foot off the accelerator and held my steering wheel as tight as I could, and that big deer jumped over the hood of my car, but the front of the car hit the mother deer and broke her legs and the little deer hit the door. The front of the car was a total loss and the left door was bent in, but our son was unharmed, a blessing from above!

These happenings made me stronger in my teachings to my family through the rough and tough times. I had a great determination to work harder for them and made sure they stayed in school. No matter what, we made sure they attended school every school day unless they were sick. I didn't keep them home for a minor cold or a headache. I gave them medicine and sent them on their way. We made sure they didn't drop out of school to go and work, or do anything that would keep them from school. I knew what it was like to have to work for others and not be able to go to school, to be denied a good education. I was determined, with the Lord's help, to give my children a better chance at life. I wanted to give them a good foundation for life.

Now was the time in my life that I had been working hoping and waiting for, to see my children graduate high school. It was something I was looking forward to because I never had that chance. It was June of 1977, our two oldest children, Zener, and Cary Jr., were ready to walk across that stage to receive their diplomas. This was a dream come true for me. If they chose not to further their education, then at least they had their high School diplomas. They had a choice, either it was college or work. Cary Jr. enlisted in the U.S. Navy and we gave him our blessings and Zener choose to work.

Our second son, Curtis, graduated in 1979, and he too chose to go to work. His first job was at the Greenwood Mills Plant in Orangeburg, South Carolina with his father. Our youngest son, Rodney, graduated in 1980 and he chose to go into the U.S. Army. He was in the Infantry Division for four years. When he left for his mission, we gave him our blessings and the Word of God to carry with him with many Scriptures marked for his comfort (like the ones below).

> *"Blessed is he that reads and those who hear the words of this prophecy, and keep those thing which are written in it; for the time is at hand."* **Revelation 1:3**

> *"He will go before you, and fight for you and to save you from your enemies."* **Deuteronomy 20:4**

These Scriptures were for his comfort when he got homesick or found himself in distress.

On visits back home and through letters, Rodney told me those Scriptures were a consolation to him, especially when he was out in the field, in that icy weather, in his sleeping bag. Yes, God's Word will give us strength!

Since I didn't have the opportunity to achieve very much education in my younger days, the word of God had been a learning experience for me. My reading ability has been greatly enriched through His Word. I am a true witness of what **Proverbs 2:6** says, *"For the Lord gives wisdom: out of his mouth comes knowledge and understanding."* With only an eighth-grade education, I have learned so much through God's wisdom.

BROTHER RETURNS HOME
CHAPTER TEN

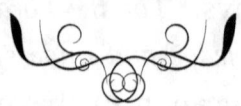

I usually work on Mondays, but this particular day, I did not. I answered a phone call giving me great news. The Office manager at the mental Institution where my brother was for more than 20 years called to say, he was being released. I could hardly believe my ears, the thing I prayed for was finally come to pass, but not without some challenges.

I remember one day I brought my brother home for a weekend visit. He had his favorite brown recliner chair he would watch TV and nod off at times. I can't say for certain a commercial was on or if something triggered him to get to the kitchen where I was cooking to strike me verbally with painful words, "Mae, you're not worth my foot to me." That was so interesting for him to say, since the feet are important parts of the body because it is your transportation, even though it is the lowest extremity on man. I realized he was striking out at me, but I'm not sure why he wanted to hurt me with his words. Maybe he wanted me to feel his pain.

I went to the door where he was standing, and I put my arms around him and said, "if I am a worthless foot to you, I will continue to be a loving worthless foot for you. He went back to his chair, and I went back to my cooking.

Moments later, Johnny came back to the door and said, "Mae, I am so sorry, I didn't mean what I said to you." I told him he was hurting and it was alright.

I was grateful for the wisdom and patience to deal with my hurting brother. I didn't fully understand then, but the Lord was working on me to do His will as it says in Philippians 2:13, *"for it is God which worketh in you both to will and to do of his good pleasure."*

September 21, 1956 until April 18, 1978; twenty-one years and seven months my brother spent his life locked away, locked out, locked down and locked up, but was finally getting his due. My genius minded brother had a mathematical mind and an exact hand for wood whittling and nothing or no one could take that away. It seemed so unfair and like it were a twenty-one and some lifetimes but life was about to change.

He was released to a rehabilitation facility for six months of intense training on life skills before integrating him back into society. He went to the Clarendon Retirement Village in Manning, South Carolina for about four months of training, and was then moved to a halfway house in Orangeburg. The halfway house was closer to our home and he stayed there for two months. Upon his release, he was very well adjusted. He learned to cook, shop, domestic work, and personal care. His skill for bed making was military style, which was better than mine. After the six-months of training, Johnny was back home with his family. It was a joyful time.

After being home for eight months, he wanted to live on his own. We started looking for apartments. He fell in love with the Orangeburg Manor apartments and when there was an opening, he moved in. He lived there for seven years with help from his family and a very close friend, Miss Loris Bridgman. They became pretty famous and cozy together. God made it possible for them to meet. She was a God send to us. I loved her as a sister.

After his seven-year tenure, Johnny moved back home and lived near me and the family where he still resides today.

UNITY
CHAPTER ELEVEN

THE NEW GENERATION – OUR CHILDREN & MARRIAGE

Love was in the air. It was one of our greatest dreams to see the children grow into adulthood, fall in love, get married and start their own generation. Cary Jr., our oldest son, was the first to marry in September 1981. The love bug struck again, this time it stung the two youngest sons, Rodney in April of 1985 and Curtis in December of 1985. Finally, the love bug stung our only daughter, Zener in August 1994. It was such a joy to know that each child made their dreams come true to have one of God's most wonderful pleasures; holy matrimony. Our family grew from four adult children to eight adult children, 12 grandchildren and 14 great grandchildren.

Family reunions, dinners and family outings are the life and fun of any family, but like in every family, there are imperfections. I just continued to pray for our children that they would not fall for the things of the world. Every marriage was not successful, but knowing they all put in a good effort with what they had, was a reward I can't take away. One main thing I desired was to keep the lines of communications open with all my children and for them to have the communication freely among themselves.

I knew that God answered prayer, and I could see that slowly and surely things were changing. Rumors stirred in our community about many things and people, and we were among the rumors, but our family survived and we are still standing today. I know prayer works.

ANOTHER TESTIMONY OF THE POWER OF PRAYER

One day I was feeling rather down and depressed. I couldn't put my finger on what was wrong with me. I sat at the kitchen table, and the Holy Spirit spoke up inside me, "Pray with your children." Two were working, so I called the two that were home and prayed with them. Later that same evening, I prayed with the other two. I still had that unrest deep down in my soul and couldn't shake it. Monday morning around 9:00 a.m., I received a call saying a young man by the name of Wade needed wrecker service. Cary had a wrecker and he went to the aid of this Wade fellow. The highway patrol didn't connect the dots. When Cary got to the scene of the wreck, he discovered it was his own son, Rodney. Although his vehicle flipped twice because a car pulled out in front of him at a traffic light on 601 Highway north of Orangeburg, he was without a scratch on his body, except his head full of glass. Prayer works and all I could say was thank you Lord!

Another incident happened while Cary and I were over hundreds of thousands of miles away from home. It was

July of 1993, we were headed to the family reunion in Sacramento, California. We left early that Friday morning to board the plane. Once in California, we had a joyful time meeting and greeting family, with high expectation of what was to come. While all excited to be in California and with family and friends, I fell asleep, but woke up from a vision. It was quite alarming. I saw my son, Cary in trouble. The car he was working on slipped from its foundation and rolled back on him, almost pinning him to the wall. He threw up both of his hands in our mechanic shop. I woke up wet from perspiration and terror. I jumped up, went to the bathroom and prayed, thanking God for taking care of our family while we were away. God is everywhere, and only He can handle any situation. I told Cary, Sr. what I experienced in my sleep and he said just what I would expect, "You prayed. Everything will be alright."

After returning home and back on the job, our son came to work that Tuesday morning and told us about the experience he had while we were away. To our surprise, some electric wires in the shop caught fire Saturday morning as he cut the lights on to start work. He went through the smoke and cut the electric box off. The electrician told him he didn't see why the shop didn't burn to the ground. It was a miracle. *If we call upon Him, He will answer.* **(Jeremiah 33:3)** paraphrased.

The dream was evident that some bad things happened. God didn't let me see the fire, but he showed me my son's deliverance with the car when I saw his hands raised. Moses had the same result when his hands were raised against Amalek according to **Exodus 17:11.**

SHOP – JOB – CHURCH AND TEMPTATION
CHAPTER TWELVE

Cary and I became entrepreneurs in 1983. Cary had many God-given talents, but his heart was in repairing cars. He started learning to fix cars at age 13 and did it from that time on. He worked for old Bossman on the farm, who saw he had a real knack for it. He started fixing cars part-time for himself, so it was a reachable goal to have his own building, his own customers, his own shop. Yes, the spirit of entrepreneurship came over Cary very strongly.

He would talk about it, dream about it, and plan for it, but I was reluctant. It's not that I didn't have faith in my husband, I didn't want to go through the ridicule we would have to face from family, and naysayers. However, his mind was made up. Cary didn't care about rumors, or challenges, he saw a dream and went for it. This was something he always wanted to do and he was willing to take a chance.

The butterflies in my stomach were real. One might think I was being a little selfish, but let's face it, we had been through so much in our lives. However, to the contrary of my worrisome soul, I gave in because I knew my husband was not going to change his mind. All I could do was support him. We stepped out on his faith, hoping for the best, but preparing ourselves for whatever came.

At this point, we were about to face some of the most trying times of our married life. Cary and I were first disappointed when we went to borrow money. Although we had good credit, we were denied the desired amount to build a large building. We had to settle for a smaller building, but he built it, a 24 x 36 foot building, a two-car garage. Cary planned to stop working at Greenwood Mills and do mechanic work full-time. During the summer of 1983 he did just that. Cary's testimony proves that God will give you the desires of your heart, even if it isn't the exact vision. Never despise small beginnings.

The building was completed and he started working in in his new mechanic shop, Wade's Auto Garage. Everything was going well for a while. Cary had good customers. We were blessed with Mr. Simpson, who helped our business in so many ways. The guys learned from each other. Simpson got me in on the deal, when I was taught how to do the monthly tax returns. We were so grateful to have him and his wife as friends.

Cary was a kind-hearted, easy-going person and enjoyed helping people, so for the first year a so, it appeared that he was giving his profits away. Statistics show that in any start up business, the first five years are the worst for seeing profit, and we were no exception to the rule. The first few years were marked by hard work with very little to no profit. There were more expenses than income because of overhead, utility bills, the cost of tools, insurance, supplies and his helper. When the monthly bills were paid, he was barely able to keep his head above water. The community went crazy! Lies started circulating, from our home church in Norway S.C. to our work place.

By people's standards, they thought a miracle had happened to us and we were in the money! It was being said, I didn't need to work. People came to our home with judgmental thoughts. I prayed, asking God to open their eyes and let them know you don't get rich by getting in debt. No one had given us anything free, and no money had fallen from the sky. We were struggling to make it day by day and week by week. My husband's good customers started leaving because of what they heard. This young woman, although she came back, stayed away for about a year, because she was told that I was carrying a gun to do women harm who came to the shop. I was at a loss for words. "Lord have mercy on the souls of whoever said such a thing."

My Granny told me to believe half of what my eyes see, and nothing I hear until it is proven. I told that young lady I was proud that my husband had good customers, and it didn't matter whether they were male or female! I am grateful for his customers that stuck by him through it all and no, I would never consider doing anything to harm anyone. Any honest person would see I love people, always have, and always will.

Next, the trouble reached my job. People started calling my job trying to get me fired by telling my supervisor to sell me a plate of wooden nickels, saying my husband was leaving with his suitcase, and for me to come home at once. It got so bad, someone told her to tell me our house was on fire. I told her if our house was on fire, my husband would have called me. Many things like this happened on a consistent basis, but I never once left my workstation.

I told my supervisor to tell them to stop calling my job and I continued praying. I knew my supervisor didn't like what was happening, nor did I. The calls made things worse on my job.

I was denied good work on my job. Many days, it was hard for me to make production doing three, five, or eight pieces in a bundle all day, when others were given, three, and four, dozen bundles so they could make their daily production. Stevie Wonder could see what was really going on, and it was not a good thing. I really needed to work to help my husband because we were in debt. I continued to pray, hoping things would change. I never thought people would turn on us as they did because of a small building and the desire of a man to do what he was born to do, but we learned the hard way.

I read in the Bible about jealous spirits, and why we see so much of it today. It started with Cain, Abel's brother. In **Isaiah 42:12**; in essence, if we don't give God the glory and the praise for one another, *He shall go forth as a might man, He will allow jealousy like a man at war.* We see it continuing in the world today! Joseph's brothers are prime examples, they had spirits of envy, hate, murder, and greed. They sold him for twenty pieces of silver). See **Genesis 37.**

The head supervisor told me to go home and work with my husband because I didn't need my job. I told her, I needed to work and help my husband, just like she had told me many times that she was working to help her husband.

I wasn't cutting it on production because they gave me less in my bundles to sew, so I got the nerve to get some work out of the bin, and the supervisor came to me saying, "You're not supposed to go to the bin to get work, what do you think you're doing?" I came back strong with, "Everybody else is coming getting work out the bin. You give me these little pieces of bundles, and I need more work." Oh, I knew she was hot with me, and she proved it when she brushed up against me to instigate a fight. My head skipped time to the three major temptations to fight in my life.

1 - When Lucille and I were children, kids would be so cruel, and I would defend her. Classmates came after me as well, so we would literally run for our lives. You may

perceive that we were scared little chickens, but Granny said it's better to be a live chicken, then a dead one. 2 - other times of a fighting spirit was with an elderly relative at church, and 3 – a young adult relative at home. I was seeing these incidents as I was in the baffling moment with my supervisor. I know I pray a lot, but I ain't a saint, and I was about to turn it back on her, but in the nick of time, I remembered Granny's words, *never turn evil for evil.*

Those words saved her from me rolling her on that floor. Instead, I just sat down and told her I knew what she was trying to get me to do, but it wasn't going to work.

As she walked away, I began sobbing. One of my co-worker who was a minister's wife came over to console me. "I saw what happened sister Wade," she said. "You are a strong woman. I am a preacher's wife, but I don't think I could have taken that." I let her know that it was just another attack of the enemy trying to make me lose my job. Even though I am aware of his tactics and devices, I didn't know how much longer I would be able to take it.

Lies upon lies spread about our finances and people believed the hype. They acted as if millions of dollars had dropped out of the air into our hands. We were being judged by what it looked like. Granny used to say, "Don't judge the book by its cover, you never know what's in it until you open it and read it."

We had thoughts of suing for slander and defamation

of character, but decided to leave it all in the LORD's hands. I can truly say as King David said…in **Psalms 109:1-5**, *"For the mouth of the wicked and the mouth of the deceitful are opened against me: they have spoken against me with lying tongues. They compassed me about also with word of hatred; and fought against me without a cause. For my love they are my adversaries: but I give myself unto prayer. For they have rewarded me evil for my good, and hatred for my love."*

Lord knows the same thing was happening to us, it was hard times for us, because I could see what was happening through my spiritual eyes. My hope came from reading God's word. It gave me strength to endure and keep on believing!

A MIRACLE DELIVERANCE FROM MY JOB

Due to all these rumors, I lived through pure torment on my job the last three years. I loved my job and my peers, and I wanted to do my best there. I was facing many offenses at this time but my hope came when I saw **Matthew 18:7** *"offenses must need be."* Lord knows, this Scripture was an eye opener for me and I began to see that many things were for His purpose to strengthen me.

I was on one operation for 13 years and doing other operations only when there was no work on my main operation. Many times, I was ready to give up and quit!

One of the head engineers would come by my machine regularly telling me my work was looking good and keep up the good work. Those words lifted my troubled mind and encouraged me to keep going.

Ambler Industries was like a home away from home, until the plant moved to its new location. The jobs were better, but things got worse and worse, especially the last three years of my tenure there. Over a period of time, the atmosphere started changing. I started having mechanical failures on my sewing machine. When I would leave at night, my machine was in mint condition, but upon return the next morning, my machine would mysteriously be broken. My question was how could it go from mint condition to failing to work? No one else used our machines, so it seemed like a conspiring joke. I had seniority and rank, but was sent home more and more for lack of work.

Sometime later, I was offered another job in the shipping department at the same plant. Seniority gave me privilege to get a new position on the job. I would get more money, but the down side was overtime and night work. I didn't take the job. I usually ask for Saturdays off. I needed the extra time with my family to organize and assist with my brother, sister, husband, and children.

Suddenly, the supervisor, said I had to be at work on Saturdays. She said, *"If you want this job, you better do like these women, and be here on Saturday."* I said, *"If it's the Lord's will, I'll try to make it,"* I replied. She came back with, "YOU BETTER FORGET ABOUT THE LORD, AND BE HERE ON SATURDAY IF YOU WANT YOUR JOB!"

I felt that I was very little help to my husband, financially. My health was failing and much of what I was making was going to the doctors. July was the vacation time and I had a goal to receive my three weeks' pay of which I well deserved after working 13 ½ years of dedicated services. Then I would vacate Ambler Industries all together with a "God bless you and good reddens!"

It was the second week in March and for two days I had great success in production. There was a rush order of garments for Sears and Roebuck to get out and my machine worked perfectly. If I needed any service, the mechanics were there on the fly. I went home feeling great and lifted because of my accomplishments. What a day, production quota with no repairs and little or no machine down time!

I returned to my job the third day, ready for the workday. I hadn't been on my station long enough to run a little piece of cloth under the needle before my supervisor called over the intercom saying, "Ethel Wade, report to the office." I said, "oh Lord, what now?" I had been called into that office so many times from one thing to another. I didn't know what to expect. I got up and made my way to her office and stood by the door. She and one of the mechanics were in the office. She informed me that my machine was broken when I left yesterday. She said, "You broke the machine again?" I hesitated, because I could not believe what I was hearing! I said, "oh no! no! no! My machine was working perfectly yesterday when I left. I even made production. We even finished that rush order." She said "yes, you broke that machine again." I repeated, "I did not break that machine. It was sewing perfectly when I left."

The mechanic held a part up in his hand, and said the machine couldn't sew without that part. I was lost for words. I realized they were not hearing anything I was saying.

She just kept saying she was tired of calling me into her office. I was surely tired of going to that office, being accused of things I didn't do! I knew I was not guilty of what I was being accused of and I wanted the head engineer to speak on my behalf. I wanted him to speak because this man would come by my machine often and tell me how good my work was and for me to keep up the good work. This engineer was one of the main reasons why I stayed on that job the last three years.

He came into the office with his head hung down. When he sat down, he didn't say anything, which was totally out of character for him. I knew in my heart something bad was wrong. After they finished talking, I told him that I didn't break the machine because it was working perfectly when I left the day before. I said, "Sir, you always said I was one of your best operators!" Then he answered me, "Ethel Wade, I have to take what my supervisor and my mechanic say." When I heard what he said, all I said was, "Mister!"

It felt like a fast ball was thrown hard and landed in my stomach, taking all the wind out of me. I was deprived of the power to move any of my limbs and my hands were locked in front of me. I was in a trance. I remember saying within my spirit, with no lip movement, "Lord, I will do whatever you tell me to do." My supervisor continued talking to me, saying "Ethel Wade, don't you look off when I'm talking to you." She repeated this many times. I could hear her, but I was unable to speak a word. Then a voice on the inside of me said, "*Go to your machine, get your belongings and get out of here.*"

Then I heard the other spirit say, "*These people are trying to take your job, go home, get your pistol and come back and do your thing!*" Then I heard again, "*Go to your machine, get your belongings and get out of here before you get in trouble.*" This had to be the Holy Spirit. The war raged between my human spirit and the spirit of righteousness. Then a rational thought came to me, and I realized that I had been on this job 13½ years; too long to lose my three weeks of vacation pay, which I desperately needed.

The evil one spoke up again, telling me to do the wrong thing, "*Go home and get your pistol, because you are being treated wrong!*" Although it was true, this was definitely going against my Granny's teaching. The Holy Spirit instructed me for the third time, "*go to your machine, get your belongings, and go home. You have a family at home who needs you!*"

When I heard the word *family*, my body became loose, and I was able to move. I didn't part my lips. I just made an about face and walked out of that office, and over to my machine, fighting hard to hold back my tears. I got my belongings and turned off the machine and walked towards three doors. From the time I left that office, I could hear my supervisor saying. "Don't you walk out of this plant, Ethel Wade. If you do, you will lose all your benefits." I kept on walking.

The first two doors were swing doors. I could hear machines stopping and my supervisor repeating herself.

What she didn't know was the benefits at that time didn't matter because I was not moving by my own power. The powerful hands of God supernaturally moved me.

The security guard was standing at the third door. He was there as inspector and informant against any woman who left with more than she brought to work. I knew He didn't have the inside scoop, but as he was reaching to investigate my belonging, an indignation rose up in me like hot coals that morning, as I said, *"DON'T TOUCH MY BAG, BECAUSE I WON'T BE BACK TO THE PLANT UNLESS MY HUSBAND CAN'T KILL ME A RABBIT OR I COULDN'T AFFORD A PIECE OF CORNBREAD."* I never stole before and today wasn't the day to be tested! He said, "You'll be back. I have seen your face many times around here. You'll be back." The security guard was trash talking, but he didn't touch my bag.

When I opened that door and I step outside, and the door closed behind me, I was free! I said, "Thank you LORD!" It is Over! God performed a miracle at Ambler Industries. A heavy burden was lifted off me. I felt as light as cotton walking to my car.

I don't remember stopping or turning at any stop lights or road signs, but I got home safe and sound.

I didn't realize how worn out my body was until I got home. My nerves suffered so bad that I had to seek medical attention. I was near a breaking point. He gave me medication but it didn't help. Cary took me to the lake. Although I couldn't swim, I could see and hear the water. I waded in the water and it seemed to calm me. God gave me a special love for water because He knew I was going to need it.

The water was my best prescription and remedy. All it took was for me to see the moving of the water. It took my mind off my problems. The water is a healing force. I probably would have had a nervous breakdown if it was not for His healing water. *(II King 2: 22) It* was a comfort to me as a blanket is to a baby.

The Lord was truly on my side. I was unemployed for more than a year, but I was able to draw all of my unemployment plus the eight-week extension, even though I had been told I wouldn't be able to draw any of it. To God be the glory.

I eventually sought part-time work, but because of prejudice, I was denied. I didn't try anymore. I did secretarial work and bookkeeping for Wade's Auto Service, my husband's professional full time job.

CHURCH

Granny had many little clever and wise sayings. One was, "*Mae, a lie will jump many ditches and get there quick, causing much confusion, but the truth takes the long road around. It goes over hills and mountains, falling down in the valley and goes through the rain and storms, but when the truth arrives at its destination, it's still the truth."*

The past was hard to overcome. I turned to the place of my solace, which was the church and my family, only to discovered that the people I was closest to did not understand me.

I walked on the church grounds one Sunday morning, speaking as I generally did to a friend who was like family to me. We shared many memorable moments of family and ministry together. We served our church for more than 27 years. As we were about to enter the sanctuary, I spoke to her with a Godly good morning, and what she said floored me, "I don't speak to troublemakers." I asked her why she said that and she just walked away. I knew she had been brainwashed and I wondered how many more of my church family members believed the lies about my family and me.

I learned that a new rumor was out about me as treasurer for the Gospel choir, they said I stole the choir money.

I was thinking I must have driven to the wrong church. The people looked familiar, but their actions and words made me feel like an ostracized criminal. As I sat in church that day I thought about a sermon that I had heard a pastor preach once. He said, "loose lips will sink a ship," and that sinking was happening to me.

Growing in the Scriptures, I learned that God's word is our judge. *(Isaiah 33:22)*

I held many positions in ministry at our church, from gospel and young adult choir president and usher board member, and finally a senior missionary. Things went well as the senior missionary for the two years, but the third year, I got no support from the church family. After everything I was going through, I needed comfort desperately, but instead, I felt I sabotaged by my church.

This little Poem says it all:

IF

Wouldn't this world be better if,
The folks we meet would say, I know something good about you" and treat us, just" that way.
Wouldn't life be lots more happier if, the good that's in us all, were the only thing about us, that folks bother to recall?
Wouldn't life be a much better blessing, if we praise the good we see, for theirs a lot of goodness in the worse of you and me.
~ Anonymous~

PROPHESY

I realized I needed stronger spiritual guidance. I had so many questions concerning my life, and no answers. I started having strange dream about Granny and the farm. She was in bed sick but didn't say a word. I also saw our mule, cow, and hogs. The hog trough was dry and there was no food nor water for them to eat or drink. The feed barn was broken. The more stress I was under, the more I had the dream. It got so bad that I decided to see a doctor, who medicated me, but it didn't stop. Cary took me back to the old homestead and we joined hands and prayed, seeking answers to that dream.

While seeking answers for that dream, I had another very annoying dream about my son and a big explosion. I awoke one morning crying as if I had been beaten. The dream was about me making three telephone calls to my oldest son. Two of the three calls were patched in to a church member. The third call was the sound of a great explosion in my ears. It sounded like trees falling.

I didn't know at that time the Lord refers to us as trees as in **Psalm 1:3** and **Jeremiah 17:8**. That dream was very frightening. I talked to Cary about it before we went to church. All through the service, I felt so troubled. When the service was almost over, tears started flowing and I could not stop them. I tried to wipe the tears because I didn't want people next to me see me cry. Suddenly, I heard in my spirit, *"tell the dream!"* I said to myself, *"Oh no. Lord no!"* I heard again, *"tell the dream to the church!"* I thought these people would think I was crazy. The more I held it in, the more the tears flowed until the water was lapping under my chin. By the end of the service, I heard again, *"tell the dream!"* I couldn't hold it back any longer so I held my hand up and asked the Pastor if he would allow me to say a few words. My heart felt so heavy as if it would burst in the cavity of my chest.

I admitted to my church that I didn't understand what was happening at the moment, but God was impressing upon me to speak. God put it on my heart to tell the people He wanted us to get closer together because we were together in body, but not in spirit.

I prayed, hoping someone would understand why I had to tell it. One of our deacons told me he felt the Lord was talking through me. Before we got home from church that Sunday, someone called one of our family members in Columbia and said I was losing my mind and that someone should check on me.

Just two weeks later, two young men who were in the church on the Sunday I spoke about the dreams, were headed toward Denmark, South Carolina when their car hit the river bridge railing, cutting the car in half, and exploding, killing them both. That same Sunday morning, one of the lead singers from the gospel choir, who was at the same service, died from a massive heart attack. As soon as we got the news, I heard in my spirit, *"That's your dream!"* I was afraid and I knew I needed help fast. I didn't understand why God showed me this vision. I knew if I didn't get answers soon, I would lose control. I prayed continually for someone to talk to about what was happening to me. I said *"Lord, I know you didn't bring me this far to leave me now, so please help me."* I confided in the pastor about the dreams and told him I sensed the leading of the Holy Spirit to teach God's word. He told me that God doesn't call women to minister or preach. WOW, that was a deep blow to me. Now I was really confused. I didn't know what to think. I was told that it was in the Bible where God said in the last days He would pour out His Spirit on all flesh, but I didn't know where to find the reference.

I went to sleep thinking about women in ministry. Under all this pressure, I began having a dream concerning darkness. The dream showed I was driving down the road in my car in pitch black darkness, unable to see anything, but I never ran off the road or ran into anything. In my sleep, I physically tried to pry my eyes open so I could see where I was going. I had this dream three times and told my husband about it twice.

The third time I had the dream, I wailed off and slapped my husband something fierce as I was trying to open my eyes. I thought he was going to sock it back to me, but instead, he said, "Ah, you need to do something now, I know you had that dream again, 'cuz you done gone to hitting me now and that ain't good." Cary and I prayed that night hoping a change was coming very soon.

The Summer of 1989

Help came to me through our small business when Sister Darby came to get her car serviced. Sister Griffin was riding with her, the two were Ministers of music at their own church. I heard so much about these two great ladies and their ministries. We started a conversation about women ministers. This conversation was just what I needed to relieve some pressure. I was blessed that day because Sister Griffin invited me to come to worship with them sometime and I gladly accepted her invitation. Cary and I didn't waste any time with our decision to worship at Greater Faith Baptist Church two Sundays a month.

The teaching and preaching were food for our souls. Our eyes were opened as we received knowledge from the Scriptures.

In the fall of 1990, I joined Greater Faith Baptist Church under watch care. However, we still served in our positions at our church as choirman and senior missionary.

Although I held on to the position as senior missionary to raise money for our church, I saw very clearly that no one supported my efforts, including my pastor.

When time came for the fundraising program, only eight people showed up, and the pastor was not one of them. I was more blessed than hurt that night, because my mind was made up to come out of darkness because there was no support at the home church.

Dr. I.V. Hilliard taught me the difference between preaching and teaching. Preaching is proclaiming the gospel and talking about it, while teaching is explaining the gospel and obtaining understanding through it.

I enjoyed the way the teaching woke my soul. After becoming a full-pledge member, I wanted to be baptized again because I didn't really understand the meaning of baptism when I was baptized in 1958. Now I knew the meaning of it because I was taught from the Scriptures. I truly wanted to bury the old man by baptism unto death, and rise in newness as I continued studying His word to become that new man in Christ. After joining the Greater Faith Baptist Church, I enrolled in the church's Baptist Bible Institute Classes.

The first class I took was entitled, "God's Word Made Plain." It was such an eye-opening experience for me. I saw the light, no more darkness, no more night. Thank God Almighty I saw His light. *Psalms 119:130 says "At the entrance of His words gives light: it gives understanding to the simple."* Yes, His word showed me the light. I realized one of the biggest missing links in my life was not being taught God's word. I learned how to think and judge righteously, which is one of the meanings of (understanding).

My second class was Memorizing the Word. We had 72 Scriptures to learn and quote by heart! This was quite a challenge and a learning experience for me. I went from no Scripture life to learning Scriptures from Genesis to Revelation. The class took us through the Bible. Sister Alfred Scott and I studied many nights until midnight learning those 72 Scriptures. We were a blessing to one another as we studied together.

The third class was Training for Service. We were

taught the books of the Bible, starting with Moses' five books of Law, the 12 books of history, and five books of poetry, etc.

I graduated from these classes with high honors and I was ready for the next class, <u>Preparing for Service</u>. Unfortunately, I never got the opportunity to take that class at Greater Faith Baptist Church because God showed me two revelations which led me to move from that place.

Making it Through Trying Times

REVELATIONS & PRAYERS
CHAPTER THIRTEEN

God gave my husband and me a love for people. We loved visiting and enjoying our families at home and abroad. We travelled many hundred miles over the years to Bradenton, Florida to visit Cary's Aunt Model and family. On our way home, we would visit his cousin Manuel Perry from Fernandina Beach, Florida.

For Christmas, in 1991, we received a gift subscription to the Daily Word devotion books from Cousin Perry, and it was a blessing I will never forget. When I received my third book, there were two great things concerning FORGIVENESS, that blessed my spirit, soul, and body.

Reference: Daily Word March Edition 1992

1- *A Self - Revelation* – An individual must realize that he or she is a spiritual being who cannot be harmed by the words and actions of others. Although the body can be slain, and harsh words can penetrate to the core of one's humanity, the true identity of a spiritual person remains untouched. This revelation identified that being a spiritual being frees one from the belief that he or she has been injured. This one really lifted my spirit.

2 - *A Realization About Others* – Other people are also spiritual beings. Atrocities can be contributed to bad things being done to you but one's spiritual nature is still intact. It may be hidden beneath hideous acts in the same way a storm shields the sun, but when the clouds pass away, the sun is still shining in all its glory. We must take heed and forgive others, if we want Him to forgive us. I remember what Jesus said on that Cross, *"Father forgive them for they know not what they do." If we don't forgive others, God will not forgive us our trespasses.* **Mark 11:26** (paraphrased).

MY PERSONAL REVELATION FROM GOD

One Wednesday afternoon before I left for church prayer service, I was cleaning around the fence near our front yard, when I saw movement in the grass. My first thought was it might be a snake, so I stood far back and took the rake and opened the grass. There was a little baby bird that had fallen from its mother's nest, breaking its little left wing. I picked him up to pray for his little spirit to return back to God, not remembering at that time, birds don't have spirits. I hid him in the grass but, I felt compassion for the little bird. Suddenly, I got a revelation from the LORD. While standing there thinking about the little bird's broken wing, I heard in my spirit *"many of my people have broken wings because they are only receiving from the New Testament.*

The little bird's wings are to fly with, but if one is broken he is not able to fly at all. The Old Testament is our Light, and the New Testament is our instruction. We need both in order to see how to follow the Testaments, which are men's wings to fly above the troubles of the world.

I was curious and wanted to know more about these spirits that I was told I had to fight. Within this same week, I met a young woman. As we conversed, she brought up the word spiritual warfare. I asked her about spiritual warfare. She gave me the name of her church, which was Ministry of Reconciliation near Orangeburg, South Carolina, and she invited me to attend a class on Spiritual Warfare. That was not by coincidence. I didn't waste any time, I got in touch with the church just in time to enroll in the class. What a blessing that was. The teaching was such an eye opener. I took three classes before deciding to join the church under watch care in 1999 and the teaching was awesome. The classes I took were:

- **Discerning Spirits**
- **Spiritual Operations**

- **Developing the New Man**

I admonish you all by the grace of God to study spiritual warfare for your family's life. Please take heed to Apostle Paul's words, *For we wrestle not against flesh and blood, but against principalities, and against powers, against the rulers of the darkness of this world, against spiritual wickedness in high places.* **Ephesians 6:12**

A PRAYER OF PROTECTION FROM THESE SPIRITS

From Psalms 91:1-6

Dear God cover us with your feathers, and under your mighty wings, we will take refuge. We declare we will not fear the enemy's attacks, no matter what time of day, or form they may take, it shall not come near our dwelling place. Only with our eyes will we see the destruction of the wicked, according to your word. We put all demonic forces under our feet.

In the name of Jesus, we come against every curse and negative word, every negative prayer, charm, chant or ritual of death and destruction. If I or any of our family members have been subjected to any of these curses, we declare each curse null and void in the name of Jesus, the Christ: (the anointed one). If any of these evil spirits have been sent against us, we decommission each evil spirit, and send them back to the Judgment of God Almighty, in the name of Jesus. We come against all white–magic, all black–magic, all Jezebel spirits, all Babylonian spirits, all Egyptian spirits, all rebellion spirits, all witchcraft spirits, and all spirits of pride. We come against all the spirits of Satanism that have been assigned to our families.

We bind each one of you evil spirits up, and send you back to the judgment of almighty God. We break your power. We cancel your assignments and your effects against us. We release the Holy Spirit in the lives of our family members. We are covered under the blood of Jesus. All thy people, and all of our possessions, we take the sword of the Spirit and disconnect every trap that Satan has set against us and we claim the victory over all tricks of the evil one, In the name of Jesus I pray this prayer, and do believe that all is well in my spirit, soul, and body. Amen.

Here is another one of my main prayers and confession: **THE PRAYER OF FORGIVENESS**

Dear Lord, as I continue sowing seeds in the Kingdom of God, I release every person who has hurt me, my family, and our business in any way. For every bad feeling, every pain, every thief, and every evil thing, I forgive them now. I ask that you will water them as you have watered me, (Proverbs 12:25) so they can water others. I lift each one of them up to you dear Lord, and I pray that these thy people will come into a greater knowledge of You, so their souls will be saved on the day of the Lord. This is thy humble servant's prayer, in the name of Jesus the Christ I pray and do believe. All is well. Amen

I have been chosen to do this work of the ministry, I will

continue to share my testimony through His Word. *"He rejoiced greatly, when the brethren came and testified of the truth that is in thee."*

I am committed to continue teaching and sharing these principles for the up-building of His kingdom. (*which are righteousness, peace, and joy in the Holy Ghost*) **Roman 14:17** For when I am weak, I am strong in Him because he has overcome the world. We can overcome in Him. Because He conquered, we are more than conquerors.

FOUR REASONS WHY WE TESTIFY!

1. *We overcome the Devil with the Blood of the Lamb, (His Word) and by the words of our Testimony;* **Revelation 12:11.**

2. He commands us to teach, preach unto the people and testify that Jesus was ordained to be the Judge of the living and the dead. **Acts 10:42**

3. Apostle Paul was pressed in the spirit and testified to the Jews that Jesus was Christ, so must we - **Acts 18:5.**

4. Testify both to the Jews, and the Greeks repentance toward God, and faith towards our Lord Jesus Christ. **Acts 20: 21**

Now we can see why our LORD says He rejoices greatly, when we testify of the truth that is in us, even as we walk in truth. **3 John 1:3,4**

EPILOGUE

My personal journal is a written document about family, happy and sad times, joy, good and bad health, but moreover, it is to show the struggle, strength, and the resolve that we win, by the almighty power which GOD gives us to fight and conquer.

We will face much turmoil in life before we learn to find joy and keep it. Joy is an internal, eternal, and supernatural emotion that can not be equated with something that happens. Although there are many stories written from cover to cover in many books about triumphs through struggles, we are still encouraged from their successes to remain joyful because we learn the power of the human spirit's ability to bounce back.

I believe joy does much more than just make us feel good, it strengthens our witness, improves our countenance, health, and our quality of life. Happiness is important in the sense that when good things happen, that emotion comes on the scene to express a good feeling.

Go on and live your best life, being fully aware that tests, trials and situations will come, but the strength of your human spirit will far exceed your resilience to get through anything.

I can do all things through Christ who strengthens me!
Philippians 4:13

Ethel G. Wade

MORE ABOUT THE AUTHOR

Ethel (Effia Mae) Gordon Wade, a minister of the gospel, radio minister in Orangeburg, native of Norway, South Carolina.

| THEN | NOW |

Accepting the call to ministry in March 1984, she remains committed to the duty of God and man. She graduated Cum Laude in Biblical studies at Greater Faith Baptist Bible Institute. She also has a Tract Ministry. You are invited to look for her tracts on her Facebook page Minister Ethel G. Wade.

If you would like to become a Christ follower, and learn the ways of joy, and find peace in the midst of all turmoil, seek the Lord through His word and prayer. For more information, please contact Ethel Wade at: ministerewade@yahoo.com

Her favorite Bible verses are *I was chosen and ordained by God,* (***John 15:16*** *Paraphrased)*, *"Chosen by God in the furnish of affliction"* ***Isaiah 48:10*** *"I was left alone to wrestle with the LORD"* ***Genesis 32:24*** and *"To be made a minister"* ***Ephesians 3:7.***

Other favorites:
Color: Royal Blue
Food: Lasagna, chocolate,
Past time: Spending time with her family, reading, and cooking.

She is grateful for His already blessed Word and is committed to spreading the Gospel to hurting generations.

She is inspired by the meaning of her name and hopes to live up to the meaning of her name: ETHEL means noble one, a treasure of the Word, genuine, caring about the interest of others, delights in the joys of others, never impatient with others.

A name is much more than just a name. An unforgettable acronym for ETHEL!

E is for Enrich, a quality you share
T is for Tried, tried and true, you
H is for Hero, as you appear to many
E is for Electric, a sparking trait
L is for LOVE, everlasting love

Ethel G. Wade

THE RELEVANCE OF THREE'S: MY TESTIMONY

*I*n retrospect, it became apparent that the number three has an extraordinary significance in my life. I have learned that other than three being the trinity of God, it is also covered in mercy, favor, and grace. Throughout the Bible, occurrences of threes can be found.

I have recalled these events to the best of my ability in chronological order, indicating God's plan, intent and purpose for my life.

- There were three children; my brother, sister and me.
- We resided on three farms with Granny, Uncle, and his family.

In 1956, my life involved three major occurrences

- My brother took sick in September
- My husband and I married in October
- My Granny expired in November
- My husband and I were blessed with three sons, one daughter.
- Between 1966 and 1984, I did public work at three plants.
- At the last place of my employment in 1984, I had to walk off my Job. However, before I departed, I spoke to three people;

- My supervisor
- A mechanic
- The lead engineer.

After which, I gathered my things from the desk and I walked out of three doors.

- In later years, I left three churches
- Saw this one vision three times.

The dream took me to Granny, lying sick in bed, seeing a snapshot of the livestock, our mule, cow, and hogs. They were hungry and thirsty. I felt so helpless because I couldn't get inside the barn to feed them because the feed barn was broken. Each time I saw this dream, I woke up feeling hopeless and depressed. During the day, I pondered the interpretation, but came up with nothing. I was left feeling bewildered.

The Lord rejoices when we testify and these three verses gave me course for the writing of my book.

- **Habakkuk 2:2** *says "Write the vision and make it plain upon tables that he may run that read it."*
- **Isaiah 30:8** *says "Go write it before them, note it in a book that it may be for a time to come."*
- **2 Corinthians 3:12**; *"Seeing then that we have such hope, we use great plainness of speech"*

As I continued receiving insight concerning the ministerial call, God showed me these three sections of

Scriptures, revealing my calling:

Numbers 12:6
Deuteronomy 18:18-20
Jeremiah 8:29

I pray you will be blessed and encouraged to persevere in your own journey while reading my story.

A DUAL CAREER CHRISTIAN MARRIAGE
Seven Principles to live by

Lesson 1

Understand men egos and treat very lightly. Ask his or her opinion even when you don't need it. There is an inner need in all human beings to feel important. Make sure you are the person filling that need in your spouse, not in "word or in tongue, but in deeds and truth." See **1 John 3:18** and **Colossians 3:18,19**.

Lesson 2

Keep the lines of communication open always, if not you will fall for anything and your purposes will disappoint. See **Proverbs 11:14; 15:22** Dual career couples must be careful not to get too caught up in their own lives, that they neglect the emotional needs of their partner; men often hide their true feelings. Women must be especially alert. See **1 Peter 5:6-8**.

Lesson 3

Never, Never, Never, never take each other for granted. **Romans 12:10** says, *"be kindly affectionate to one another in truth."* Note of thanks, praise, and appreciation for things done to help one another above and beyond the expected. They are just as important at home, as in the workplace... "speaking gracefully." See **Colossians 4:6**.

Lesson 4
Always plan time for fun. Look at your weekly schedule to make sure you can allow time for each other. Have fun together, and lie not to one another, always be truthful to each other. See **Colossians 3:9.**

Lesson 5
After your business trip, don't hit the door with the words I'm exhausted. Remember that your spouse may have had a difficult week also. "Do all things without complaining and disputing" See **Phil. 2:14.**

Lesson 6
If your career takes you to higher heights, compass your spouse and remember it's not your money, or my money, it's our money. For any successful partnership, God's word says, *"let them do good, that they be rich in good works, ready to give, willing to share."* See **1 Timothy 6:18**

Lesson 7
When your career in blooming, and your ego is full of self-satisfaction, it's easy to forget the important things in life. Don't forget who will be there for you when you are old, certainly not your coworkers, your boss, nor the CEO. Don't forget your family, and remember family ties are made to be forever.

FOUR MARRIAGE TIPS TO REMEMBER

1. **Always communicate:**

Know you can't handle conflict if you don't communicate. You must get things out in the open. You must be able to say, I love you, but I don't like the way you behave.

2. Give each other space

There are times when each partner needs time for themselves – whether to go out with a friend or just to do something that may not interest you.

3. Recognize your own shortcomings

Some tend to withdraw, saying, "I am going to cool down, and then we can talk." No! Sort things out quickly. Granny always said a stitch in time saves nine stitches, meaning work on the problem before it gets too large; do something about it right away.

4. Work toward a common goal

Relationships are constantly changing, but if you have a goal you both want to reach, it will help to work out other problems that will arise. Whether your goal is spiritual or natural, work together. Young couples should expect bumpy patches in their relationship. Bumpy patches help smooth the path ahead, and makes it easier to accept disappointments.

Reference: Lisa R. Silberstein – 1992

SIX STEPS TO SALVATION

Take heed to these six steps of salvation, and our children can overcome these sins through sanctification.

Salvation Has Six Steps
- Acknowledging
- Repenting
- Confessing
- Forsaking
- Believing
- Receiving

- Acknowledge~ acknowledge in the light of God's Word: that you are a sinner. *"For all have sinned, and come short of the glory of God." "If we say that we have no sins, we deceive our, ourselves the truth is not in us."* **(1 John 1:8)**

- Repent~ Realize the awfulness of sin: and then repent of it... *"Except ye repent, ye shall all likewise perish. Repent ye therefore and be converted, that your sins may be blotted out."* ... **(Acts 3:19).**

- Confess~ Confess, not to men, but to God: *"If we confess our sins, he is faithful and just to forgive us our sins, and to cleanse us from all unrighteousness."*
"With the mouth confession is made unto salvation."
(Romans 10:9,10)

- Forsake. Sorrow for sin is not enough in itself: We must

want to be through with it once and for all. "Let wicked forsake his way and unrighteous man his thoughts and let him return unto the Lord...for he will abundantly pardon." (Isaiah 55:7)

• Believe. Believe in the finished work of Christ: on that cross. (John 19:30) *"For God so loved the world that he gave his only begotten Son, that whosoever believeth in him should not perish, but have everlasting life."*
To be sanctified, set apart, and covered under His blood, we must take heed to ourselves and these Doctrines (parables and short stories from the Scriptures).

• Receive ~ And receive Christ personally into your heart by faith: Proverbs 23:26 - and know He "says, *"But as many received Him, to them gave He power to become the sons of God, even to them that believe on His Name."* John 1:12.

By doing so you, will save both yourself and the ones that hear you. **1 Timothy 4:16**

Now I can see clearly ~ SALVATION ~ Is being able to overcome evil with good. He says, "And I, if I be lifted up from the earth, I will draw all men unto me." John 12:32 As MOSES lifted up the fiery serpent in the wilderness and the people that looked on" and lived. Today as we look on God's word, we will save both ourselves, and the ones that hear us! (1 Timothy 4:16)

Dear ones, the purpose of my life story, it is to lift Jesus up, show how His great love toward mankind saved my life many times over, and give me a mouth of Wisdom: ~LUKE 21:15 ~ and He will do the same for you.

Now, why should we deny our fellow man the love, that he or she craves so deeply? Let us learn to give, receive, and express love, generously, honestly, and graciously! "Giving glory and praises to the LORD, in the land." Avoid the spirit of jealousy. **(Isaiah 42:1,12,13)**

To be sanctified, set apart, and covered under His blood, we must take heed to ourselves and these Doctrines (parables and short stories from the Scriptures).

By doing so you, will save both yourself and the ones that hear you. **1 Timothy 4:16**

www.ingramcontent.com/pod-product-compliance
Lightning Source LLC
Chambersburg PA
CBHW051948290426
44110CB00015B/2158